Henry VIII
Tudor Serial Killer

His victims and their stories

By

Gerard Batten MEP

"The handsomest potentate I have ever set eyes on…so gifted and adorned with mental accomplishments of every sort that we believe him to have few equals in the world." Venetian Ambassador, Pietro Pasqualino 1509

"The King is a beast, and worse than a beast." Sir Edward Neville 1538

www.BretwaldaBooks.com
@Bretwaldabooks
bretwaldabooks.blogspot.co.uk/
Bretwalda Books on Facebook
First Published 2014

Bretwalda Books
Unit 8, Fir Tree Close, Epsom, Surrey KT17 3LD
info@BretwaldaBooks.com
www.BretwaldaBooks.com
ISBN 978-1-909698-95-6

Printed and bound in Great Britain by
Marston Book Services Ltd, Oxfordshire

Contents

Introduction

It is a cliché, but nonetheless true, to say that Henry VIII is the most famous King in English history. Even those who care little about our history if called upon to name just one English king could probably cite Henry, and indeed pick him out in an identity parade if shown Hans Holbein's iconic portrait. Henry's larger than life character still looms over us even after five centuries. Indeed, we still live with the consequences of the momentous decisions he made. He arguably did more to shape English society than any other single monarch.

Many distinguished historians have studied his life and times and written marvellous works about him. There are probably more books about Henry than any other English monarch. So why write another one? This book started as a casual remark to my publisher, Rupert Matthews. I asked him what he thought of a little book that would list all of Henry's victims and the reasons why they were executed. I expected him to tell me to forget it as it had all been done before, but instead, he invited me to write it. So many months later, here it is.

Many books about Henry look at his life from the perspective of his six marriages; but I wanted to look at him from the perspective of those he killed. It did inevitably mean looking at his state of mind, his health, and the most important events of his reign, to try and explain why his victims met their deaths. It took longer to write than I anticipated as the list of the beheaded, the hung-drawn-and-quartered, and those burnt at the stake, kept on growing. It ended up with many more than the usual well known names we are familiar with. Even so, space does not allow it to include the names of all Henry's victims, and for that I apologise to them and the reader.

I have tried to tell these peoples' stories and to convey something about their lives and personalities as best I could. Many of those executed on Henry's orders still live in the popular imagination: Anne Boleyn, Catherine Howard, and Thomas More, to name just three. Their ghosts still stalk our historic imaginations.

Recently, I met a Yeoman Warder at the Tower of London. He remarked to me that the Tower was 'the most haunted place in England'. I asked him if he had any personal experience of this.

He answered 'Yes'. He told me how, when he was new to the Tower, and living in one of the apartments reserved for the Warders, he had been woken at 2am in the morning: someone or something was lifting up the foot of his bed…. Who might it have been? There is a long list of suspects to choose from.

Gerard Batten, London, June 2014.

Chapter 1
Was Henry VIII
a psychopath?

A woodcut of Henry in heavy armour by the Dutch artist Hans Liefrinck.

Henry VIII's reign could not have begun with more promise. Ascending the throne just two months short of his eighteenth birthday he was described by the Venetian Ambassador Pietro Pasqualino as: *"The handsomest potentate I have ever set eyes on; above the usual height, with an extremely fine calf to his leg, his complexion very fair and bright, with auburn hair combed straight and short in the French fashion, and a round face so very beautiful that it would become a pretty woman, his throat being rather long and thick. Not only very expert in arms, and of great valour, and most excellent in his personal endowments, but likewise so gifted and adorned with mental accomplishments of every sort that we believe him to have few equals in the world."*

By his death thirty eight years later Henry had turned into a feared and bloated tyrant, with a long toll of victims dispatched under a legal system that can only be described as judicial murder. The scale and nature of his killings has led some modern academics to ask if he was a psychopath.

What is a psychopath? Sadly, we are all too familiar with the psychopathic serial killer in modern society. A serial killer is defined as someone who has murdered three or more times. Henry certainly qualifies on that simple criterion; but he was not a criminal murdering on some kind of compulsion. All of his judicial murders had a reason behind them, albeit as a selfish means of getting his way, or because of political considerations coloured by his increasingly paranoid view of the world.   But was he a psychopath?

While many people may have psychopathic personality traits few actually end up killing people, still less on a serial basis. But what constitutes a psychopath? The Canadian psychologist Robert D. Hare formulated a twenty-point check list for psychopathic behaviour. This is summarised below. Although it is designed to be used in a modern context with regard to criminal behaviour one can see that many of these character traits are readily attributable to Henry:

1) Glibness and superficial charm
2) Grandiose sense of self-worth
3) Need for stimulation and proneness to boredom
4) Pathological lying
5) Cunning and manipulation
6) Lack of remorse or guilt
7) Shallow emotions, despite apparent gregariousness
8) Callousness and lack of empathy
9) Parasitic lifestyle
10) Poor behavioural control
11) Promiscuous sexual behaviour
12) Early behavioural problems
13) Lack of realistic long-term goals
14) Impulsivity, foolhardiness and rashness
15) Irresponsibility, failure to honour obligations
16) Failure to accept responsibility for one's own actions
17) Many short-term marital relationships
18) Juvenile delinquency
19) Revocation of conditions of release (e.g. parole conditions)
20) Criminal versatility

It is apparent that Henry possessed quite a few of these traits. He had great charm and powers of manipulation, and an enormous sense of his own self-worth.

He consistently seemed to lack remorse or guilt for his actions. That said, he certainly did not lack long-term goals when he needed them. He persevered with his divorce from Katherine of Aragon against great obstacles; and when thwarted in that by the Pope, he showed single-minded determination in creating a political and social revolution that not only overturned the power of the Catholic Church in England but created the foundation of England as a truly independent nation state; an outcome that enabled its success on the world stage for the following four hundred years.

Dr David Starkey, one of the foremost experts on Henry summed up his personality thus: *"He was intelligent; his memory was good, and his eye for detail sharp. He was a shrewd judge of men and had a flair for self-projection and propaganda. Moreover, he was both ruthless and selfish, while his staggering self-righteousness made him proof against doubt and the dark night of the soul."*[1] This assessment does not make him a psychopath; but certainly sounds like summary of many of the key characteristics needed to qualify. Another academic, Professor Kevin Dutton, carried out a study in 2013 on ten of the most famous people in English history to assess if they fitted the criteria for a psychopathic personality: of the ten considered, only Henry VIII provided enough evidence to be considered a true psychopath.

Professor Dutton's book, *The Wisdom of Psychopaths* [2] was inspired by the psychologist William James who theorised that the most successful people in history were likely to show the kind of personality traits common to psychopaths. When ranked against a 'psychological spectrum' designed to identify those traits Henry scored 174 points against a psychopath ranking that starts at 168. Henry *"scored very highly for emotional detachment and cold-hearted ruthlessness, both characteristics of dangerous psychopaths"*. Other characteristics shared by psychopaths are: Machiavellian self-interest, persuasiveness, physical fearlessness, emotional detachment, rebelliousness,

8

feelings of alienation, carefree spontaneity, and coolness under pressure; most of which Henry showed in abundance.

Although Henry scored high in the ranking it is possible to score even higher. More dangerous tyrannical leaders spring quite easily to mind who make excellent subjects for study: Joseph Stalin, Adolf Hitler, Mao Tse-tung, to name just three who killed on an industrial scale without regret or remorse. Henry was certainly nowhere close to their league; but he did become more dangerous and unpredictable as he grew older, possibly, at least in part, due to his medical conditions and the considerable pain he suffered from, as well as in response to the changing political circumstances.

We can easily see how some of Henry's psychopathic traits were displayed in the events of his life. As a nineteen year old he allowed his father's faithful servants, Empson and Dudley, to be sacrificed, although their only crime had been to obey his late father's orders in taxing his nobles to the hilt to accrue the enormous fortune that young Henry now had the leisure to spend. Henry permanently removed some of those with a better claim to the throne than him, because they might prove a threat to his stability, or that of his heirs.

Likewise he could sacrifice a long-standing friend like Sir Thomas More, or a respected churchman like Bishop John Fisher, without compunction. In all fairness it has to be said that these actions were not taken out of impulse but because his victims stood in the way of his overriding goal of marrying the woman he loved (or thought he did) and ensuring the continuation of the Tudor dynasty.

The most shocking example of Henry's cold-blooded ruthlessness and lack of remorse is the way in which he removed Anne Boleyn and her co-accused on trumped-up charges of adultery, incest, and treason. One of the co-accused was his friend Sir Henry Norris who had been one his inner circle and trusted companion since his coronation. Equally shocking was the way he executed the harmless 67-year-old Margaret Pole,

Countess of Salisbury, for no better reason than he could not lay hands on her son who was safely on the Continent.

As Henry grew older he also grew more suspicious and turned on those around him. When his most faithful fixer and hatchet-man, Thomas Cromwell, failed him, and had grown too powerful, Henry executed him too. He later regretted it, not out of remorse but only because he realised he had lost the 'the best servant he ever had'. Cromwell carried out Henry's orders not only very effectively but without the least compunction. Henry may have felt however, and with some justification, that Cromwell had manipulated him. Henry could never allow himself to be controlled by anyone.

Henry's early life was somewhat unusual for a royal prince. He was brought up by his mother with his sisters in the tranquil atmosphere of Eltham Palace near Greenwich; meanwhile his elder brother Arthur, the heir to the throne, had been as was the custom, installed in his own household with his own retainers and servants. Henry's beautiful mother Queen Elizabeth died when he was twelve years old and he must have felt that keenly. He received the best education that could be provided, not least benefiting from the tutelage of Sir Thomas More. His love of, and skill in, music and composition must also have originated at that time.

On his brother's death in 1503 he became the heir to the throne. His father kept him close by and restricted his movements so that he could not go from his own chamber without first passing through that of the King. He would have been aware from his earliest years that he enjoyed a completely different status from ordinary human beings. That would be enough to turn the head of anyone, let alone someone with psychopathic personality traits. Nonetheless in his teens we hear that he loved the tournament and would come and observe the jousts, talking with the knights and commoners involved to feed his thirst for knowledge of the sport but without compromising his dignity as heir to the throne. He had the charm of the common touch when he needed it.

After ascending the throne he was the subject of endless flattery and praise. He could do no wrong, and when wrong was done it must be someone else's fault. Even his victims at the block had to maintain the fiction and thank him for his mercy in order to try and mitigate the effects of his anger on their families. Dr David Starkey says that there were two Henrys: young Henry and old Henry. Old Henry comes into being around 1536 when he was forty-five years and his health started to seriously decline. The vast majority of his executions came after that time and continued unabated to his death. But why so?

Henry's search for romantic love in marriage had produced nothing but loss and bitter disappointment. The golden days of his youth when he had delighted in being with his nobles eventually gave way to fear and loathing of them and what they might be planning. From 1537 his dynasty depended on his one legitimate son, Edward. By the early 1540s he must have feared he did not have long for this world and knew the dangers his young heir would face when he was gone.

He executed the young Henry Howard, Earl of Surrey, on flimsy accusations of treason despite the fact that Surrey had been the childhood friend and companion of his much loved and deceased illegitimate son, Henry Fitzroy. Henry's last wife, Katherine Parr, lived in fear of the death warrant; and his oldest surviving henchman the Duke of Norfolk, Surrey's father, only escaped the executioner because Henry died before he could sign his death warrant.

Henry showed in abundance the psychopathic character traits that made his executions possible. His sense of grandiose self-worth meant that he could not be to blame when things went wrong. When he tired of Anne Boleyn it must have been because she had 'bewitched' him. He allowed himself to believe Cromwell's lies that she had been unfaithful to him with her own brother and sundry others in order to get rid of her. His bluff exterior and great personal charm were shallow and he could show enormous cruelty, callousness and lack of empathy with those he consigned to their deaths, even lifelong friends. He only too famously had many short-term marital relationships, and was sexually promiscuous throughout his life.

In Henry's defence let it be said that he did not execute all of those of the old aristocracy who might pose a potential threat to his crown. He acted every inch the King, but he knew enough about aristocratic genealogy to know there were many alive who, in the right circumstances might take it on themselves, or be used by others, to claim the throne. He knew that the Tudors had a slight right to the throne and that his father had achieved it by right of conquest. The example of Richard III showed that in the space of a few hours a proud armoured king, mounted on a white horse amid his army, could be transformed into a butchered and bloodied corpse lying in the mud, with the crown plucked from a bush to be placed on another's head. Henry had no intention of meeting that end, or visiting it on his heirs because of any weakness in asserting his authority.

If he did not start out as a paranoid he certainly has some justification in becoming one. His court was a seething cauldron of different factions and personalities, plotting, planning and manipulating for their own preference and advancement in anticipation of his death and the threats and opportunities that would give rise to. And as he became older and weaker he almost inevitably became more ruthless in protecting his dynasty. If Henry VIII did not have a psychopathic personality then he certainly came very close. The reader can consider the stories of his victims and their deaths and make up their own minds as to how many of the psychopathic character traits Henry possessed.

Chapter 2

Henry's Health: Illnesses, Conditions and Injuries

Henry's health is of great interest because it may have affected his ability to produce a healthy male heir, and his mental state and behaviour. The medieval world was a dangerous time to live for anyone, and being of high rank offered little extra protection. Childbirth was a great danger to women, and infant mortality was high. Conditions were insanitary for all, and various contagious diseases and plagues were common. The quackery practiced by the medical profession was as likely to kill as to cure.

In 1502 Henry's older brother Arthur died at the age of 15, probably of pulmonary tuberculosis [3]. Henry's father Henry VII died at what would now be considered the relatively young age of 52, also probably of tuberculosis. His mother Elizabeth of York had died in 1503 at the age of 38 of childbed fever. Henry VIII contracted smallpox at 23 and recovered.

At the age of 30 he contracted malaria, a not uncommon disease in England at that time, and he suffered from recurring bouts for the rest of his life. In his late thirties he suffered from varicose veins; and in later years from constipation, due no doubt to his unhealthy diet.

Henry was originally intended for a career in the Church and he was highly educated and enlightened in many ways, with a wide variety of interests. He was a skilled musician and a composer of music still played today. He had a lifelong interest in medical matters and founded the Royal College of Physicians in 1540 by amalgamating the two existing companies of barber surgeons. His Parliaments passed seven different Acts licensing and regulating medical practitioners. Henry was conscious of his health and presided over the making of medicines and ointments for himself and friends. Despite the various illnesses it was difficult to avoid in 16th century England, Henry remained relatively healthy until his mid forties.

Henry was tall even by today's standards, being well over six foot. His surviving suits of armour allow us to chart his body changes. In his youth he was slim waisted at 34 inches with a chest of 39 inches, and weighed about 15 stones. By the end of his life his waist had expanded to 52 inches, his chest to 53 inches, with an estimated weight of about 28 stone. In youth he was athletic and delighted in his martial and sporting prowess being skilled in jousting, fighting on foot, archery, tennis and wrestling, as well as being a lover of dancing. But his masculine and virile image was not matched by his ability to father healthy children.

Henry's first wife, Katherine of Aragon had six pregnancies. Two babies were stillborn, two died after a few hours, one boy, Henry, lived for fifty-two days, and one girl, Mary, survived into adulthood and inherited the Crown. In 1519 Henry's mistress Bessie Blount gave birth to a son, Henry Fiztroy. Henry's second wife, Anne Boleyn became pregnant three times, firstly bearing the future Elizabeth I, followed by two miscarriages. His third wife Jane Seymour gave birth to the future Edward VI, who died aged 15. Henry's wives and mistresses are known to have had eleven pregnancies.

Anne Boleyn gave birth to their daughter Elizabeth on 7th September 1533; and probably suffered a miscarriage in July 1535. Anne's third pregnancy ended on 29th January 1536 when she miscarried after hearing the news that Henry had suffered a serious jousting accident and his life was at risk. The child reportedly, *"had the appearance of a male"*. Henry was not infertile and produced four surviving children that we know of: two females that survived into adulthood, and two boys who died in their teens. Henry was extremely proud of his illegitimate son Henry Fitzroy and genuinely loved him. Fitzroy died suddenly aged seventeen in 1536 of unknown but natural causes - to Henry's great grief.

In recent years two American researchers Dr Catrina Whitley and Kyra Krammer have advanced the theory [4] that a medical condition may have been responsible Henry's lack of offspring. They contend that Henry was 'Kell Positive', a rare blood type that causes serious fertility and health problems; as well as possibility of causing the related genetic disease known as 'Mcleod's Syndrome'.

A Kell negative mother who becomes pregnant by a Kell positive father usually carries the baby to the full term but each subsequent pregnancy is at risk. Katherine of Aragon gave birth to their first child, a still-born daughter just seven and a half months after their marriage, so presumably it was premature. Their second child was a boy but he was sickly and died after fifty two days. They were luckier on 11th February 1511 when Katherine gave birth to their daughter Mary, who later reigned as Mary I (1553-1558). Thereafter no children survived. Fertility was obviously not Henry's problem; but genetic incompatibility between the father and mothers may be have been the problem.

The associated genetic disorder of McLeod's syndrome usually becomes apparent between the ages of thirty to forty. The symptoms include muscle weakness, depression, personality disorders, paranoia, and even schizophrenic-like behaviour. The symptoms become progressively worse with age leading to late-onset dementia. Such symptoms might possibly be attributable to Henry except that there are other symptoms that he did not display; for example, irregular muscle contractions, facial tics, and lip and tongue biting. There is insufficient evidence to reach a conclusion if Henry suffered from these conditions but if his body were exhumed modern forensic science might resolve the issue.

Diabetes

There are a number of similarities between Henry and his maternal grandfather King Edward IV. Edward was a renowned warrior, exceptionally tall, well built, handsome, charming, and when the occasion required, ruthless. He executed his own brother George Duke of Clarence for treason in 1478; although it has to be said not without severe provocation. Not having any problem producing legitimate heirs with his Queen, Edward was also promiscuous, with a number of mistresses and illegitimate children. Like Henry he was fit and healthy in his youth; but in the last few years of his reign he suffered from ill-health, put on a great deal of weight, and died at the young age of forty-one in 1483. The symptoms he displayed have given rise to speculation that he may have suffered from diabetes, a disease with an heredity element.

It is possible that Henry suffered from Type 2 Diabetes. This is a disorder of decreased insulin secretion and gives rise to a number of complications. These may include: heart attacks, strokes, sight failure, and kidney failure. It often causes poor circulation, which may then result in the increased likelihood of infections and the slow healing of wounds. Henry's problems with his leg ulcers indicate osteomyelitis, an infection of the bone, which is also a common complication of diabetes. Diabetes is made worse by obesity, poor diet and inactivity, all factors in the last decade of Henry's life. Interestingly, Henry's sister Margaret also suffered from strokes and mental decline in her later years. Diabetes is treatable today by tablets or injections but in Henry's time the disease was not even understood let alone treatable.

Leg Ulcers

In 1527 at the age of 36 Henry is reported to have suffered his first ulcer, which appears to have affected his thigh, and he was laid up in Canterbury with a *"sorre legge* (which leg we do not know). One of his personal physicians, Thomas Vicary was called to his aid and the ulcer healed. In gratitude the King appointed Vicary as Sergeant-Surgeon on an annual salary of 20 shillings.[5] Henry's life-changing jousting accident of 1536 may have caused fractures to one or more of his bones; although they initially healed, ulcers later appeared that affected him for the rest of his life.

The ulcers were particularly unpleasant. They seeped pus and gave off a foul stench. They caused bouts of fever, and it is recorded that the King was on occasion, "*without speaking, black in the face and in great danger.*" [6] The doctors' treatment according to the teaching of the time was to keep the ulcers open to allow drainage, and they did this by lancing them with red hot irons – and that in the age before any kind of anaesthetic. One can only imagine the effect on Henry's mood and temper. The ulcers never healed properly and in March 1541 it is recorded that Henry was again laid low with fever.

The ulceration of Henry's legs may have been due to sporting and jousting injuries and given rise to deep vein thrombosis. An article in the Journal of the Royal Society of Medicine in December 2009 offers the explanation that the grossly swollen legs that Henry suffered from towards the end of his life represent 'congestive cardiac failure in an arteriopath' and contributed to his death.

Another possibility is that an injury to his legs caused underlying bone damage leading to an infection, or osteitis. Chronic osteitis if unhealed would be tender and painful and would lead to bouts of fever which we know Henry suffered from. The condition also poisons the system, causing a waxy material to be laid down in the liver and kidneys, which would no doubt contribute to Henry's other health problems.

Syphilis

A popular theory is that Henry may have suffered from syphilis or the "*great pox*" as it was known then. If Henry had syphilis then who did he catch it from? An interesting theory is that he could have caught it from his first wife Katherine of Aragon. [7] After the death of her teenage first husband, Prince Arthur, Katherine was alone and kept in relatively poor circumstances by her father-in-law Henry VII. In her years of loneliness (1502-1509) she became attached to her confessor a Spanish Franciscan monk named Diego Fernandez.

Fernandez was allegedly a character of low morals and the Spanish Ambassador reported this, and their closeness, to her father the Spanish King. Fernandez remained in the Queen's household for some years as she refused to give him up. Eventually however Fernandez was convicted of fornication and dismissed from office. Could their relationship have gone too far? This seems unlikely given Katherine's intense and sincere religiosity. Perhaps she looked on him in similar way that the Tsarina Alexandra looked on Rasputin, seeing a saint where others saw a dirty old devil.

If Henry did have syphilis then he would have infected others. He had three mistresses we definitely know of: Elizabeth Blount who produced his son Henry Fitzroy; Mary Boleyn, Anne's elder sister; and Margaret Shelton, Anne Boleyn's cousin. There were most likely many more. As far as we know, none of Henry's wives or mistresses displayed the symptoms of syphilis; neither did his surviving children, Edward VI died young at 15, most likely of pulmonary tuberculosis; Mary probably of a malignant ovarian tumour; and Elizabeth of old age and pneumonia. The main treatment of syphilis then was the administration of mercury, something poisonous and damaging to the body in its own right. There are no records of Henry or his doctors purchasing mercury.

Injuries

Being a sporting man of action Henry inevitably suffered a number of injuries. In 1527 he injured his foot while playing tennis. The resulting swelling caused Henry to wear a single loose fitting black velvet slipper on the injured foot. His court of sycophants adopted the same fashion until the injury healed.

A more obscure accident is recorded as having happened in 1524 or 1525 near Hitchin in Hertfordshire. One of Henry's great pleasures was hunting, including hunting with hawks. The hunters would follow their hawks on horseback, and when conditions required they would dismount and hunt on foot. On one such hunt Henry is said to have pursued his bird on foot and impetuously pole vaulted a ditch: *"In this yere the kyng folowyng his hauke, lept over a diche beside Hychyn, with a polle and the polle brake, so if one Edmond Mody, a foteman, had not lept into the water, and lift up his hed, whiche was fast in the clay, he had bene drouned; but God of his goodness preserved him."* [8]

Edmund Mody or Moody, from Bury St Edmunds in Suffolk, was born around 1495, and was one of the King's footmen, the lowest rank of person on the hunt. His quick thinking and action may well have saved Henry's life; he could easily have suffocated with his head stuck firmly in sticky mud under water. Henry was certainly grateful and rewarded Edmund with a pension of £6 per annum, a not inconsiderable sum. Edmund was also made a Knight and granted a coat of arms. The motto Edmund chose was "*The Reward of Valour.*" How different English history would have been if Henry had drowned in a ditch aged 34.

But the most dangerous of Henry's activities was jousting; and he suffered two significant accidents, one in 1524, and the most serious in 1536. Jousting began in the middle ages as a means of knights practising for battle. Initially extremely dangerous, over time it evolved into a highly regulated spectacle designed to minimise the risk to the participants. Mounted knights rode at each other along either side of a wooden barrier that prevented their horses colliding. They wore specialised armour that was much heavier than ordinary armour designed for warfare.

The silhouettes of Henry's jousting armour show the way his body became fatter as time progressed.

Henry was a great connoisseur of armour and patron of armourers, setting up his own armouries in Greenwich. Various suits of his tournament and jousting armour survive, and apart from displaying the genius of the armourer's art, give a record of his expanding girth over the years. A suit of jousting armour might weigh as much as 120 pounds compared to 60 to 90 pounds for a suit of field armour.

Shields were no longer in use and instead, the left side of the armour were made much thicker in order to take the full impact of the opponent's lance. Helmets were designed to minimise the risk of the lance or its splinters entering the eye slit. By Henry's time the intention was not to unseat an opponent but rather to score points by a direct hit on his left side. This was demonstrated by 'breaking a lance'. Blunted lances were of hollow construction so that a direct hit would result in its breaking into pieces.

Despite the safeguards jousting was still dangerous. Henry's accident of 1524 was described by George Cavendish, Gentleman-Usher to Cardinal Wolsey. Cavendish describes how the King had a new suit of armour designed to his own specifications for a joust on 10th March at Greenwich. His opponent was his old friend Henry Brandon, Duke of Suffolk. The Duke being told by an attendant that the King had come to the end of the tilt, he set off at a gallop with his lance levelled. The King seeing this charged too, in the excitement not realising that his visor had not been lowered and his face was bare. The crowd seeing the danger shouted for them to stop but both thought the crowd were cheering them on and the Duke's lance struck the King on this helmet.

Cavendish describes how the blow struck the King on his right brow of his helmet below the upturned visor and how the splinters of the lance flew into his face. He was lucky not to be blinded or killed. The impact had been taken on a part of the helmet normally covered by the visor and of which Cavendish tells us the armourer *"takes no heed"*, presumably because it was not intended to take an impact in the normal course of events with the visor lowered. Brandon was mortified but the King was remarkably philosophical about it and blamed no one but himself. Henry then ran another six courses of the joust to prove he was unhurt. However from this time on he suffered recurrent headaches.

On 24th January 1536 Henry suffered a much more serious jousting accident. He fell to the ground, and his heavily armoured horse fell on top of him. The impact was comparable to forty mile an hour head-on car crash. He was unconscious for two hours, and his servants thought that he might die. Today a head injury resulting in only five minutes of unconsciousness would be regarded as serious. We don't know the details of how he was unhorsed: did he perhaps suffer another impact to the head? Or was his loss of consciousness a result of his horse falling on him? He suffered concussion, and possibly injury to the frontal lobe of the brain, which can result in marked personality and behavioural changes and loss of inhibition. Henry may also have sustained further injuries to his legs that resulted in the ulcers that plagued him henceforward.

The news of his accident was given to Anne Boleyn and the fright of hearing his life was in danger, and the precariousness of her own position were he to die, may have been the cause of miscarrying what would have been their son on 29th January. Whatever the effect the injuries had on Henry, within six months she was beheaded.

As Dr David Starkey has said, the young and old Henry were two completely different personalities. Whether this was due to brain injury, the effects of continued pain, or merely his underlying personality traits having to deal with increasing problems we cannot say, but certainly he became more unpredictable and his tendencies to vindictiveness and cruelty were more apparent from this time onwards.

Lifestyle

After his jousting accident of 1536 Henry's mobility became gradually more restricted. He could no longer joust or play tennis although he could still ride considerably distances and continued his love of hunting, but his leg ulcers became worse and his continual weight gain meant that in his final days he had to be carried around in a chair.

Anne Boleyn, one of the first victims of Henry's increasingly vicious nature after his jousting accident of 1536.

have led to problems with circulation, requiring his heart to work harder and to high blood pressure, all of which no doubt contributed to his demise.

Death

Henry died at about 2am in the morning of 28th January 1547 at his palace in Westminster. He was relatively young at just 56 years old. A non-medical opinion might conclude that he died of the cumulative effect of his various illnesses, injuries and lifestyle. In his book *A Medical History of the Kings and Queens of England*, Clifford Brewer states the likely of death as renal (kidney) and hepatic (liver) failure. It is possible that a forensic examination of his remains could throw valuable light on the nature of his afflictions, and possibly the exact cause of his death.

Always a hearty eater, in his misery he resorted to comfort eating and he consumed vast amounts of food, particularly meat, pastries and wine; a diet that resulted in bouts of chronic constipation. He is estimated to have eaten around 5,000 calories per day, twice that for an active man of today. His increased weight would

Chapter 3

Like Father Like Son: Judicial Murder

The Tudors did not have a strong claim to the English throne. Henry Tudor Earl of Richmond was descended from royalty on both sides, but by illegitimate lines. His grandfather, Owen ap Marredudd Tudor, was a Welsh adventurer who fought at Agincourt, and had been appointed as the Clerk of the Household of Henry V's widow, the French born, Queen Catherine of Valois. After Henry V's death in 1422 Queen Catherine was retired to the gilded cage of Leeds Castle in Kent. Her nine months old baby son was proclaimed Henry VI and she was forgotten about.

Some years later when the King's officers checked on her wellbeing it transpired that she had fallen in love with Owen and had a number of children by him. Unfortunately the course of true love did not run smooth

Henry's father, King Henry VII, is crowned on after winning the Battle of Bosworth in 1485.

for the lovers. The behaviour of Queen was frowned upon and she had to take refuge in a convent in Bermondsey. Owen sought the protection of Henry VI, which he received, and he fought on the Lancastrian side in the Wars of the Roses. He was taken prisoner and beheaded after the battle of Mortimer's Cross.

King Henry VI obviously thought it was not becoming for him to have several illegitimate half-brothers and sisters and he legitimised and enobled them by Act of Parliament. Owen and Catherine's eldest son Edmund Tudor (1430-1456) was made Earl of Richmond in 1452. For reasons best known to himself Henry VI decided in 1455 that Edmund should marry Lady Margaret Beaufort.

Lady Margaret Beaufort (1443-1509), who was just twelve years old at the time, was heiress to an immense estate. She was descended from John of Gaunt, third son of Edward III and his mistress and true-love Katherine Swynford. The couple had four illegitimate children and were married in 1395 after the death of John's wife, Constanza of Castile. Immediately after their marriage John petitioned the Pope to recognise the legitimacy of any pre or post-marriage children, and the Pope duly obliged. In 1397 Gaunt's nephew Richard II, equally obligingly confirmed in Parliament, in an unprecedented decision, that the

offspring were legitimate and entitled to inherit any rank, status or property, "... *as fully freely and lawfully as if you were born in lawful wedlock…*"

Richard II was deposed in 1399 and the new king, Henry IV, his cousin, ascended the throne. In 1407 he confirmed the legitimisation of the Gaunt children but with one qualification: he inserted the words, "*excepta dignitate regali*" – 'excepting the royal dignity'. The Beaufort children (named after the castle in France where they were born) could inherit anything from their father except the English Crown. Whether Henry IV had the authority to retrospectively change the decision of Richard II in Parliament was debatable; but it was through his Beaufort ancestry that Henry Tudor later claimed the throne of England. [9]

By 1455 Lady Margaret Beaufort was sole heiress to the family fortune, and quite a catch. Her twenty-five year old husband Edmund could not wait to consummate the marriage and consolidate his claim on her inheritance, and made his child bride pregnant without delay. She gave birth to Henry

Tudor aged thirteen in 1457, and was lucky to survive. The traumatic birth wrecked her chances of having any more children, and Edmund died the same year. Margaret married twice more, but her formidably energies and intelligence were focused on advancing the fortunes of her son; opportunities for which she was ever watchful.

As members of the House of Lancaster, Margaret and her son were on the losing side in the Wars of the Roses. The House of York held the throne under Edward IV (1461-1483), and Richard III (1483-1485). Henry was prudently sent into exile in Brittany in 1471. During the reign of Edward IV, Henry Tudor had been a minor irritation whose claim to the throne had no serious champions among the nobility; even so, Edward IV would have liked the opportunity to part his head from his shoulders, but Henry evaded his clutches.

The minor irritant however became a major threat in late 1483 when it became widely believed among the nobility and populace alike that Richard III had murdered the Princes in the Tower.

Even in that turbulent and violent age child-murder was beyond the pale. By right, Margaret Beaufort's claim to the throne preceded that of her son; but no woman had ever held the throne in her own right. The last time it had been tried in 1135 it has resulted in nineteen years civil war. Margaret's ambition was for her son not herself, and she conspired with the discontented and ambitious nobility in England to bring Richard down and replace him with Henry.

At the age of twenty-eight, after fourteen years of exile, trials and tribulations, Henry Tudor, sponsored by the King of France, invaded England with a small force of supporters and mercenaries. He defeated and killed Richard III at the Battle of Bosworth, 22nd August 1485. The thirty-year-long Wars of the Roses had not been three decades of sustained warfare, but rather a serious of intermittent, campaigns fought between the aristocracy and their private armies.

It is calculated that the actual amount of time spent on the various campaigns and battles was not more than fifteen months in total. The vast majority of the population were untroubled by the dynastic struggle taking place. The wars did not deplete the ranks of the nobility to as great a degree as is sometimes stated; but it is notable that at Bosworth Richard III was joined by only four peers of the realm (two of whom betrayed him), and Henry by only two. Most of the nobility wisely stayed out of the fight waiting to see which side won, and most likely with little enthusiasm for either.

Having been proclaimed King, Henry VII's troubles were not over. He faced challenges from two imposters, Lambert Simnel in 1487 claiming to be Edward Plantagenet Earl of Warwick, the imprisoned nephew of Edward IV; and more seriously in 1491, when Perkin Warbeck claimed first to be the Earl of Warwick, and later Richard Duke of York the younger of the Princes in the Tower. The last battle in this saga was fought at Blackheath, now a suburb of south London, in 1497. Simnel was a mere child manipulated by others and never a serious contender; he was put to

work in the Kings' kitchens and died in service as a falconer to Henry VIII in 1525. Perkin Warbeck was more credible and posed a more serious threat.

There were other genuine members of the nobility who had better claims to the throne than the Tudors. One such was Edward Plantagenet 18th Earl of Warwick (1475-99), the son of George Duke of Clarence, who had been executed for treason by his brother King Edward IV in 1478. The young Edward was well treated by Edward IV and likewise by his uncle Richard III; had Richard been quite the monster of Shakespeare's play then we might have expected him to have done away with young Edward in 1483 along with the Princes in the Tower, but he did not.

Edward's claim to the throne was stronger than Richard's as his father was the middle brother and Richard the younger; but his father had been attainted and he had technically lost the right of inheritance. When Henry VII became King he inherited the problem of the ten year old Edward and what to do with him. He put the problem on hold by imprisoning him in the Tower of London. Henry VII was a conventionally religious man and blatant murder, especially of a child, was not for him. He liked to do things by the letter of the law; he was not going to murder his rivals as Richard had done. Instead he used the methods of trumped-up charges and the legal process to secure executions, thereby salving his conscience. But all said and done, this was nothing more than judicial murder.

Henry VII kept the young Earl of Warwick in strict confinement with no education or mental stimulation, deliberately in order to dull his wits and make him less of a threat. It was said that the result of his long imprisonment from childhood made him almost an imbecile, and as a contemporary chronicler commentated, *"He could not tell a goose from a capon"*. Edward's misery had ended on 24th November 1499 when he was beheaded at the age of twenty-four on trumped-up charges of trying to escape his imprisonment in league with the imposter Perkin Warbeck. Warbeck had been placed in confinement with Edward and a phoney escape plan engineered to entrap them both. Henry then literally killed two birds with one stone. Henry VII set the scene and created the precedents for judicial murder to be used much more extensively and with much more enthusiasm by his son.

Empson and Dudley 1510

Sir Richard Empson was the son of a wealthy citizen of Towcester, Northamptonshire. He trained for the bar, became an MP, and then Speaker of the House of Commons in 1491. He was made a knight in 1504; was appointed High Steward of Cambridge University, and Chancellor of the Duchy of Lancaster. **Edmund Dudley**, born around 1462, was also a lawyer and a privy-councillor. He was the author of an absolutist and long forgotten political tract entitled *The Tree of Commonwealth*. Both were employed by Henry VII as collectors of taxes, fines and penalties due to the Crown, and in common with most tax collectors, they were heartily disliked by the unwilling subjects of their attentions.

Two of Henry VII's key policies had been to break the power of the aristocracy and to squeeze as much money out of them as possible. In both he was extremely successful. Unlike his more warlike royal predecessors he pursued a policy of peace in order to keep as much of his accumulated revenues as possible. Henry VII was not as miserly as is sometimes said, he knew the value of spending in order to keep up the appearances of kingship but he did not waste money unnecessarily. He was most at home in his counting house counting out his money. In modern parlance Henry VII was a micro-manager who kept the exercise of power closely in his grasp; to carry the modern analogy further, he governed the country as a combination of Managing Director, Finance Director, and Chief Accountant all rolled into one. When he died he left behind an estimated £1.8 million [10] pounds in his treasury, a colossal sum at the time.

Following his victory in 1485, Henry took steps to ensure that the aristocracy could not rise against him in rebellion later. He outlawed the keeping of private armies by the nobles (Statute of Liveries); he did not make new peers to fill the gaps left by the Wars of the Roses; he demoted some peers to a lesser rank (who were no doubt relieved to keep their heads); and rode roughshod over the ancient constitutional liberties of the land. He enacted a law, contrary to Magna Carta, that empowered Justices of Assize and of the Peace to try all cases, except those of treason, without a jury.[11] Although to his credit, Henry VIII repealed this law on his accession.

Henry VII raised money from the aristocracy (and anyone else who had it) by various means including: Benevolences, or forced loans (see Glossary); the extractions of fines and penalties for infringing his laws; and by whatever other means his tax collectors excelled at devising. Those who tried to evade giving loans (or rather donations since they were never repaid) were caught on what became known as Morton's Fork (named after Bishop Morton one of Henry's earliest supporters). If they lived lavishly they were deemed to be rich enough to pay, if they lived frugally then they were deemed to have the savings with which to pay – there was no escape.

The nobles were kept in check by means of 'Bonds'. These bonds took the form of an agreement with the King, with financial penalties for non-compliance. Some bonds were to guarantee the payment of a debt to the King, some were to ensure the successful performance of an office; but many were open-ended in form, and the judge of the successful compliance of the bond holder was the King. By the end of his reign, an estimated two thirds of the nobility had been the subjects of such bonds. The administration of these bonds was the work of a committee called the Council Learned at Law, and the dominant members of that committee were the King's lawyers, Empson and Dudley.

Small wonder then, that when Henry VII died on 21st April 1509 it was an immense relief to the nobles and the wealthy; all the more so since his successor Henry VIII, who was just two month short of his eighteenth birthday, was seen as offering a new golden age totally removed from the dismal parsimonious reign of his father. Like many a new ruler he began by endearing himself to those who felt themselves badly treated by the previous administration. Henry VIII's new Council saw something of a resurgence of the power of the nobility, whom he engaged with and involved in his government.

His new Council set up various commissions of Oyer and Terminer (To See and Determine - see Glossary) to investigate the various infringements of the Magna Carta, and breaches "*of the laws and customs of our Kingdom of England*". [12] Henry shrewdly asked all people with claims or grievances against the Crown to come forward and voice them. His Council was inundated with complaints and petitions. This

Margaret Beaufort was Henry's grandmother and a dominant influence on his early life.

the late King's excesses, perhaps hoping to excuse themselves. They defended themselves on the grounds that all they did was strictly legal. Sadly for them, and not for the last time, was the defence that they 'were only carrying out orders' rejected. They were convicted and beheaded on 17th August 1510 on Tower Green.

The nobility had their revenge. Henry VIII began his reign as a new broom sweeping clean, but nevertheless he kept the money in his father's treasury and set about spending it with enthusiasm. Henry had from the beginning shown that deft understanding of brutality and public relations that he kept for the rest of his life.

provided a safety valve to allow grievances against the old king to be aired while allowing to the new king to get off to a fresh start.

Not least of the complaints were those against Henry VII's principle tax collectors, Empson and Dudley. They were arrested and tried on charges of constructive treason. In true show-trial fashion they gave a frank statement of

Chapter 4
The Destruction of the Old Nobility: the de la Poles, and the Duke of Buckingham

Although not a wholesale destruction, the early part of Henry VIII's reign did see a winnowing of members of the old aristocracy who might pose a potential threat. The victims were members of the de la Pole family who were descendents of the House of York by means of the sister of Edward IV; and the Duke of Buckingham who was a descendent of Edward III.

To avoid confusion it needs to be explained that the de la Pole family was different from the Pole family who appear later in this book. The Poles were descended from George Duke of Clarence whose daughter Margaret married Sir Richard Pole. The de la Poles and Poles were cousins on their Plantagenet mothers' side.

John de la Pole, Duke of Suffolk, had married to Elizabeth Plantagenet, sister of King Edward IV. They had three sons:

John (Earl of Lincoln), Edmund, Richard and William, and a daughter, Anne who became a nun. **John, Earl of Lincoln**, had been named as successor to Richard III when his own young son and heir died in 1484. Lincoln fled to the court of his aunt the Dowager Duchess of Burgundy. He joined forces with the small invasion force of Lambert Simnell. He was killed when their force was defeated at the battle of Stoke, 16th June 1487.

Edmund de la Pole, 6th Earl of Suffolk

Edmund surrendered the Dukedom of Suffolk in 1493 and accepted demotion to an Earldom. He served Henry VII loyally at the Battle of Blackheath in 1497 against the mercenary army of Perkin Warbeck, but this did not save him. Feeling increasingly threatened he fled abroad in 1499 to seek refuge with his

Aunt Margaret, Duchess of Burgundy. He returned, then fled again in 1501. In exile he sought the protection of Ferdinand of Spain but became a diplomatic pawn, and was surrendered to Henry VII in 1506, when he was imprisoned in the Tower.

In 1513 there were rumours that King Francis I of France was about to recognise Edmund as rightful King of England. Henry VIII was about to embark on his invasion of France and ordered Edmund's immediate execution for treason. Henry's excuse was that his brother, Richard was fighting on behalf of the French enemy. Edmund was beheaded for treason in April 1513. This was without doubt a cold-blooded judicial murder. Henry fully realised the danger posed by the claim of the de la Pole family to the throne, and when be embarked for war in France he could not afford to leave Edmund behind as a potential rallying point for rebellion.

As it turned out the threat was real enough. The Scots, the traditional allies of the French and enemies of England, launched their own invasion of England as soon as Henry left the country; only to be catastrophically beaten at the Battle of Flodden 9th September 1513 by an English army led by Thomas Howard, Earl of Surrey. Howard was subsequently restored to his family's Dukedom of Norfolk (this Thomas was the father of the Thomas Howard, 3rd Duke of Norfolk). The Scottish King James IV, Henry's brother in-law, was killed along with his illegitimate son, twelve earls, fifteen lords and heads of clans, and eight or nine thousand soldiers. It was a Scottish national disaster.

Edmund's brother, **Richard**, who was known to his supporters as the White Rose and styled himself the Duke of Suffolk, was meanwhile safely in exile on the continent. He enjoyed considerable prowess as a soldier of fortune, selling his skills to France and other European powers. He died fighting on the side of the French King at the battle of Pavia in 1525. When news of his death reached Henry VIII he reportedly triumphantly (and prematurely) exclaimed, "*All the enemies of England are gone!*" Henry then ordered that the messenger be given more wine. [13]

Sir William de la Pole

William, the youngest brother, was born in 1478. He was lord of Wingfield Castle in Suffolk, a picturesque moated manor house, which still exists today. William married Katherine Stourton in 1497; she was already twice widowed and, aged about forty-two, over twenty years older than William. The marriage may have been one of convenience since she was wealthy having been left property by her second husband Lord Grey, and they had no children. Little is known of William but he seems to have been arrested and imprisoned by Henry VII in about 1501 when Edmund de la Pole fled abroad for the second time.

William's imprisonment in the Tower of London continued under Henry VIII for an incredible thirty-seven years. He died sometime between October and November 1539 at the age sixty-one. His was the longest imprisonment of anyone in the Tower. Although some prisoners were kept in reasonable accommodation and could pay for their own luxuries, others were held in dark, cold, damp cells. We don't know how William passed his time and in what conditions he lived, but his incarceration for almost two thirds of his life was inhuman. We don't know if he died of natural causes or was murdered; but it is more evidence of Henry VIII's callousness that he could keep someone locked up for that length of time, ageing and forgotten. We cannot say that Henry murdered him, but he was responsible for his dying alone and forgotten in the Tower.

The de la Poles were judicially murdered, driven into exile, and imprisoned for life for the simple reason that they had a greater right to inherit the throne of England than the Tudors and while they remained at liberty or alive they represented a real or potential threat.

Edward Stafford, 3rd Duke of Buckingham

Stafford was an old style aristocrat born in 1478. His father, Henry Stafford, 2nd Duke of Buckingham (c1454-1483) had been Richard III's right-hand man in his seizure of power in 1483. In his book *Richard III*,[14] Paul Murray Kendall posits the theory that it was Buckingham who was responsible for the murder of the Princes in the Tower. The theory goes that Buckingham's encouragement of Richard to depose the princes and usurp the throne was the first stage in an elaborate plot orchestrated by Henry Tudor's supporter Bishop John Morton (c1420-1500) and Margaret Beaufort. The Princes having been deposed in June 1483 Buckingham had them murdered and rose up in rebellion against Richard. Having removed them from the scene and pinned the blame on Richard, Henry Tudor would be made King and Buckingham would become the second most powerful man in the kingdom.

It is certainly a mystery as to why Buckingham rose up against Richard, having already been well rewarded for his support; possibly he had designs on the throne himself; but the revolt in the autumn of 1483 was a dismal failure and Buckingham was quickly captured and summarily executed, Richard calling him the, "*The most untrue creature living*". There is no proof to support Kendall's theory, but after the failed rebellion Morton fled into exile to be with Henry, and Margaret Beaufort was lucky to escape with her life. Richard was certainly not as ruthless as his Tudor successors, who would undoubtedly have had Margaret's head. Henry subsequently appointed Morton Archbishop of Canterbury in 1486.

A portrait of Henry Stafford, 3rd Duke of Buckingham by an unknown artist, possibly painted after

The hook to hang the theory on is Buckingham's aristocratic sense of entitlement and grievance. He was descended from Thomas of Woodstock, the youngest son of Edward III. Both his grandfather and his father had been killed fighting on the side of Henry VI and the Lancastrian cause. Edward IV's Yorkist victory had seen the twelve year old Henry Stafford made the ward of Edward's IV's Queen, Elizabeth Woodville; he was later forced into marriage with her sister Katherine. He despised the upstart Woodvilles and no doubt felt gravely aggrieved at his forced association with them, which was beneath his rank. His life is obscure until he bursts onto the scene for his short-lived and ill-fated career in power politics during 1483.

His son **Edward Stafford**, the **3rd Duke**, was restored to the family honours, forfeited under Richard III, by Henry VII in 1485. Edward's preoccupation in early life was to restore the Staffords' power and wealth in South Wales and the West Country, and this kept him from court. Although his family's history was as firm supporters of the Lancastrian cause (even more so if there was any truth in the conspiracy theory) his aristocratic lineage and link to royal blood would nevertheless make him an object of suspicion to the Tudors. He ought to have trod extremely carefully, but he did not.

Henry VIII's ascent to the Crown saw, to a degree, the restoration of the influence of the old nobility, with many of them, including Buckingham, summoned to Court. Unlike his father, Henry VIII wanted to be surrounded by his nobles, at least in the early days. Two of the highest nobles at court were Buckingham and the Duke of Norfolk. But they were very different characters. Thomas Howard 2nd Duke of Norfolk had worked his way back to favour and adapted to the new politics of the Tudor court; he was, like his son the 3rd Duke, a survivor who made alliances irrespective of his personal feelings. Buckingham was an old-school aristocrat, proud and unbending.

Buckingham was thirteen years older than Henry, and while a member of this inner court, as befitted his rank, he never hit it off with him. Stafford resented and despised the new men at court of inferior rank who became the King's counsellors; and if the truth be told, probably despised the upstart Tudors. The bad blood between Buckingham and Henry seems to have begun with a personal issue very early on in 1510.

Buckingham's sister Anne was a lady-in-waiting to Queen Katherine. Anne was, it seems, romantically involved with Sir William Compton, a close friend of the King. She may also have become involved with the young Henry during his wife's pregnancy. So the story goes, Buckingham found out about the affair and confronted Compton and reputedly said to him, "*Women of the Stafford family are no game for Comptons', no, nor for Tudors' either*". [15] This caused a row between Henry and Buckingham which resulted in Anne being sent away from court. Henry had been embarrassed in front of his own Queen and court, and he was, no doubt, aware of Buckingham's aristocratic resentments.

Henry VIII's initial slackening of the tight grip on power kept by Henry VII saw the rise of factional politics in the court between the nobility and the growing power of Cardinal Wolsey. Wolsey was a remarkable self-made man who became the second most powerful man in the realm. His meritocratic rise to power cut no ice with Buckingham who resented him as an upstart commoner, Cardinal or not. Once in a public ceremony when Buckingham was holding a basin for the King to wash his hands Wolsey impudently dipped his hands into to it, the Duke then deliberately spilt water on the Cardinal's shoes: a contemptuous mark of disrespect that Wolsey did not appreciate or forget.

Buckingham survived until 1521 but he made himself a marked man by various indiscretions. Most seriously he was reported to have lamented the execution of the Earl of Warwick in the final years of the reign of Henry VII. Worse than that, he said, God was punishing the King for his father's misdeeds, "*by not suffering the King's issue to prosper, as appeared by the death of his sons*". [16] Wolsey collected these and other reports, true or false, and related them to the King. As Henry and his Queen consistently failed to produce a male heir there were mutterings as to who might lay claim to the throne when Harry passed on, and Buckingham's lineage put his name in the frame.

The Duke was arrested and tried by his peers on trumped-up charges; he was not allowed to question witnesses, and inevitably found guilty of treason. The record of his sentence has survived and reads that he was to be, "*laid on a hurdle and so drawn to the place of execution, there to be hanged, cut down alive, your members to be cut off and cast in the fire, your bowls burnt before you, your head smitten off, and your body quartered and divided at the King's will, and God have mercy on your soul.*" Fortunately for him Henry mitigated the sentence and he was beheaded on 17th May 1521. His lands were then distributed among nine peers.

His greatest crime was being directly descended from Edward III. He lost his life because of his potential claim to the throne through his lineage, and because of his opposition to Wolsey. Wolsey was not a man to oppose. The Holy Roman Emperor, Charles V, is reported to have said, "*A butcher's dog has killed the finest buck in England*": a reference to Wolsey reputedly being the son of an Ipswich butcher. But Henry VIII had shown again that he could ruthlessly take the life of someone who he thought might become a threat. He also sent out an unmistakeable signal to the nobility of who was boss.

37

Chapter 5
The Break with Rome

Let us break off from the bloodshed for a while to consider the events that led to the next spate of protracted judicial murders. Had Henry and Katherine of Aragon been the proud parents of a just one or two healthy male heirs it is almost certain that Henry would never have broken with Rome, and England would might never have become the firmly Protestant country it did in the reign of Elizabeth I.

There may well have been friction between the Royal and Papal authority in England, and possibly even calls for some 'repatriation of powers' to use a topical phrase, but until his most basic need to produce a legitimate heir was thwarted by the Pope's refusal to grant him a divorce, Henry would remain a firm and conventional catholic monarch; indeed Henry proclaimed he was a catholic until he died, according of course to his own rather elastic interpretation of what that meant.

Queen Katherine of Aragon by Lucas Horenbout, a Flemish artist who was an official court artist from 1525 to 1544.

By 1527 Henry had resolved to divorce his wife Katherine of Aragon and replace her with his sweetheart Anne Boleyn, out of personal preference and in order to produce a male heir to secure his dynasty. Divorce as such was not possible under the Catholic Church but annulment was. These were often granted, especially to deserving nobility and monarchs. Annulments were usually granted for unconsummated marriages or where the blood relationships between the partners were found to be too close. In the age of dynastic marriages the partners of the nobility were often related and dispensations were required to allow marriages to proceed; unless the marriage was blatantly incestuous dispensations could be procured.

If the marriage later failed for whatever reason an obliging bishop might find a technical fault in the original dispensation by which the marriage would be found never to have been valid in the first place. The down side of such an arrangement was that any children produced would be illegitimate. This was the route Henry sought with the Pope. What he hoped would be a simple if perhaps lengthy process inadvertently resulted in a religious and social revolution in England.

When the process began, Henry had no intention of breaking with Rome. He had no time for the doctrines of Martin Luther and indeed in 1521 he had been awarded the title of *Fidei Defensor* 'Defender of the Faith' by Pope Leo X (Giovanni de Medici) for his book defending the sacraments of the Church against Luther's doctrines. No doubt in 1528 he expected Pope Clement VII (Giulio di Giuliano de Medici, and Leo X's cousin) to return the favour and grant him his annulment.

In the normal course of events Pope Clement would no doubt have been happy to oblige a doctrinally friendly monarch like Henry, but he had a problem. The most powerful monarch in Europe was Charles V, King of Spain and Holy Roman Emperor, and Katherine of Aragon's nephew. Charles strongly objected to his aunt being set aside in this manner and his cousin Mary being declared a bastard. In 1527 Charles had besieged the Pope and ransacked Rome in one of the most disgraceful episodes in European history. Poor Pope Clement lived in fear of Charles; and his safety, and that of Rome, was a far higher priority than solving Henry's marital problems.

Henry may have considered freeing himself from Katherine as early as 1519 when it was growing apparent that she would not produce a healthy son, and when he had proved himself capable of fathering an illegitimate healthy son with his mistress Bessie Blount. It may have been Wolsey who planted the idea in Henry's mind that his marriage was unlawful on the basis of the Bible passage in Leviticus C20:V21 *"And if a man shall take his brother's wife, it is an unclean thing: he hath uncovered his brother's nakedness; they shall be childless"*.

Leaving aside the obvious, that it was his brother's wife's nakedness Henry had uncovered rather than his brother's, he nevertheless took the teaching to heart and became convinced God had denied him children because of an invalid marriage. Henry had indeed applied to the Pope for a dispensation to marry his brother Arthur's widow in 1509 on the basis that their marriage had never been consummated, and which Pope Julius II had gladly granted. If Wolsey did plant the idea of divorce in Henry's head he must have come to regret it for it was to prove his downfall.

By 1527 Henry had resolved to marry Anne Boleyn and he needed a solution. His request for an annulment had been delayed as long as possible by Pope Clement who had so far avoided making a decision on the matter. Initially he had suggested to Katherine that she enter a nunnery and leave Henry to take his case to the English ecclesiastical court, if they found in his favour the verdict could then be appealed to Rome. Katherine would have none of it, and neither would Henry: if he married Anne, produced a son, and then Rome had found against him he would be in a worse situation than before. An heir declared a bastard by Rome would be a recipe for future rebellion and civil war. Clement finally had to take some action and in 1528 he sent his representative Cardinal Compeggio to England to set up a court to try the validity of the marriage.

Compeggio arrived in October 1528 but the Legatine Court was not convened until 31st May 1529 at Blackfriars. Compeggio obviously had Papal orders to delay the matter as long as possible and the court provided a golden opportunity for theological pedants to have their say and counter say. Katherine made an appearance but instead of recognising the authority of the court made an emotional appeal to Henry himself. She stated that she had been a true, dutiful and faithful wife and swore that on their marriage she had been a virgin, and concluded with *"And whether this be true or no, I put to your conscience"*. With that she curtseyed to the King and left the court. Henry notably never accused her of lying on the matter of her virginity at their marriage. The court was expected to deliver its verdict on 23rd July but instead Compeggio announced that the court would be adjourned for the holidays until 1st October.

In her book *Bastard Prince, Henry VIII's lost son*, about the life of Henry Fitzroy, Beverly Murphy raises a very interesting point. The dispensation that Henry applied for in 1509 when he sought to marry Katherine was for 'affinity'. This was required when one of the applicants had, had sex with a member of the other's family. The implication was that Katherine and Arthur had consummated their marriage. That not being the case, the correct dispensation to have applied for was for 'public honesty', which recognised betrothal or marriage but that no consummation had taken place. Since Katherine categorically denied consummation, and Henry did not contradict her, he could have sought an annulment on the technical grounds that they had sought and obtained the wrong type of dispensation and it was invalid in the first place. Instead Henry chose to fight on the moral high ground of Levicticus, with the inherent contradictions in his argument in that he would have to call his wife a liar, and which he would not do.

Henry learned that the Pope, under pressure from the Emperor, intended to call Compeggio back to Rome for the decision to be taken there. Henry decided he would wait no longer and decided on another course of action. He accepted the advice of Thomas Cranmer, a Cambridge cleric, that he should seek the opinion of the universities of Europe on the question of the validity of his marriage. With the failure of his policy to gain a Papal annulment, Cardinal Wolsey was dismissed from office.

His place was taken by his even more unprincipled and unscrupulous protégé Thomas Cromwell. The verdicts of the universities were not unanimous but a majority found in favour of Henry's case. Meanwhile, Henry called a new Parliament filled with his yes-men and which was intended to diminish the power of the clergy in England and put increasing pressure on the Pope to comply.

The Church had enormous power and wealth independent of the King. It owned vast amounts of land and property, paid taxes directly to Rome, and had separate ecclesiastical courts. All matters were divided into spiritual or temporal. The spiritual courts of the Church worked under their own law and their own procedures, and with powers of appeal to Rome. All clergy were exempt from the jurisdiction of the temporal courts. The temporal courts worked under the Common Law, and as we have said had no jurisdiction over the clergy. The centuries-old monastic system represented almost a state within a state and controlled vast wealth and economic power.

Cromwell demonstrated his worth by initiating his strategy to destroy the power of the Church step by step. In January 1531 the whole of the clergy were indicted for treason under the law of Praemunire. The laws of **Praemunire** had been enacted under various English kings during the 14th century. Blackstone defines it as *"introducing a foreign power into the land, and creating imperium in imperio* (a government within a government)"*. Richard II had introduced refinements which stated, *"whoever procures at Rome, or elsewhere, any translations, processes, excommunications, bulls, instruments, or other things which touch the King, against him, his crown, and realm, and all persons aiding and assisting therein"* were guilty under the statute. The clergy were allowed to purchase their pardon from Henry for the then colossal sum of £118,840, many hundreds of millions at today's prices.

The Convocation of Canterbury in May 1532 saw the process of the **Submission of the Clergy**, and the loss of their power to formulate church laws without the King's licence of assent. The King addressed the Convocation and said, *"Well beloved subjects we thought that the clergy of our realm had been our subjects wholly, but now we have well perceived that they are but half our subjects, yeah, and scarce our subjects; for all the prelates at their consecration make an oath to the Pope, clean contrary to the oath they make to us, so that they seem to be his subjects and not ours. The copy of both oaths I deliver here to you, requiring that invent some order, that we be not deluded of our spiritual subjects"*.

The Convocation deliberated until, under great pressure, the King's articles were signed by some of the bishops, but not all. These articles were that, canons (church law) could not be made without the King's licence and consent, and that no church canons could be made that were contrary or repugnant to the Royal Prerogative, or the customs, laws and statues of the realm. This included all canons already in place.

In 1532 Parliament passed the **Act of Restraint of Annates** which abolished the system by which the Pope received first year's income of all newly appointed Bishops and Archbishops. In 1533 Henry finally lost patience with the Pope and married Anne Boleyn on the 25th January, on the basis that he was never legally married to Katherine of Aragon in the first place.

In March 1533 the **Act of Restraint of Appeals** was passed by Parliament by which all bishops would henceforward be appointed by the Crown and all recourse and appeals to the Bishop of Rome (the Pope) would be illegal. Henry was made the ultimate legal authority in all religious matters. Meanwhile Thomas Cranmer, who had been appointed as Archbishop of Canterbury in March 1533, declared that Pope Julius II's dispensation for Henry to marry Katherine had been invalid. The Act prevented Katherine from taking her case to Rome; it named Henry's children by Anne to be his rightful heirs, thereby making Princess Mary illegitimate.

On 5th April 1533 the Convocation of Canterbury meeting at St Paul's Cathedral in London, decided that Henry and Katherine's marriage was against divine law and nothing the

Pope could say would make any difference. Twenty-five clerics voted against, including John Fisher Bishop, of Rochester who was promptly arrested. [17] On 10th April, Archbishop Cranmer confirmed Henry and Anne's marriage, and Anne's coronation was arranged for 1st June.

In 1534 Pope Clement at last gave his long awaited ruling on the royal marriage and declared it to be valid. Henry was therefore bigamous and threatened with excommunication. This was a red rag to Henry's bull and he carried on disengaging England from Papal jurisdiction with renewed vigour. There was now no going back. November 1534 saw the **Act of Supremacy** passed by Parliament which fully established the break with Rome and a repudiation of the Pope's power in England. The Act declared that the power of 'headship' of the English Church was God-given to the king and had been usurped by the Pope in previous centuries. Henry declared himself Head of the Church of England.

There was something in this argument. Certain powers over the English church had been surrendered by William I in order to gain the Pope's support for his conquest of England in 1066. King John had fallen foul of the Pope because of his various crimes and he had been excommunicated; and consequently his subjects owed him no duty of allegiance. In order to remove the excommunication, and fear of rebellion, he was forced on 15th May 1213 at Dover castle to surrender his crown to the Papal legate and received it back as a fief of the Holy See. He was now the Pope's feudal liegeman and bound to pay an annual tribute, he was no longer the sovereign lord of England.

The arguments about sovereignty and jurisdiction rumbled on through the centuries. In 1366 King Edward III's parliament declared that a king only held his kingdom in trust for his successors and could not surrender sovereignty without the people's consent, consequently the transaction between King John and the Pope had been unconstitutional and void. This was one of a series of anti-Papal statutes enacted by various Plantagenet kings that sought to limit the power of the Pope in England, which, as discussed above, culminated in the act of Praemunire in the reign of Richard II (see Glossary).

Henry's marital dispute was just the inevitable next stage in the contest. Henry might not have a strong legal case about the headship of the Church but the real argument was: could there be two sources of power and authority in one state, and the English answer in 1534 was a firm '*No*'. Henry's son-less marriage and his desire for Anne Boleyn were just the catalyst that brought it to a head. The Act of Supremacy declared that Henry "*his heirs and successors, kings of this realm* (was/were) *the only Supreme Head in earth of the Church of England...and shall enjoy...all honours dignities... immunities, profits and commodities to the said dignity.*" All references to the Bishop of Rome were to be erased from the prayer books. [18]

This was followed by the **Treason Act** 1534 which extended the legal definitions of treason. It was now treason, punishable by death, to '*will, desire or attempt in any way bodily harm to the King and Queen or their heirs; deprive them of their titles or estates; say or publish in any way the view that King was a heretic, schismatic, tyrant, infidel or usurper*'.[19] The **Act of Succession** 1534 required officers of the Crown and certain others to recognise and swear loyalty to the issue of Henry and Anne's marriage. Thomas More and Bishop Fisher declined to do so and were sent to the Tower.

On 7th January 1536 Katherine of Aragon died; but by then it was too late to undo what had been done and Henry had no inclination to do so. He had achieved sovereignty in his own nation and he was not going to relinquish it. He was however keen to show that his argument was with the Pope and not with the doctrines of the Catholic Church as such. In 1537 he ordered the publication of *The Bishop's Book or the Institution of a Christian*

Man in which he reiterated all the doctrines of the Catholic faith without the headship of the Pope.

However the growing popularity of the New Learning, and Lutheranism, posed a threat to Henry's view of Catholicism in England under his headship and this prompted him to require Parliament to pass the *Act Abolishing Diversity in Opinions* (Statute of the Six Articles) or the *Bloody Statute* as it became known, in June 1539. The Six Articles in question required everyone to believe in certain fundamental tenets of the Catholic Church. These were summarised as:

i)   Transubstantiation: the real presence of Christ in the Eucharist (communion bread);

ii)   That the laity should only receive communion bread at the mass;

iii) The unlawfulness of the marriages of priests, and that they should be celibate;

iv)   The obligations of the vows of chastity on all who took them;

v)   The propriety of maintaining private masses;

vi)   The need of the confession of sins to a priest.

The sentence for rejecting the six articles was death; but it is thought that only twenty-eight people suffered the death penalty during Henry's reign, [20] a modest amount by contemporary standards.

While all this was going on Thomas Cromwell had been busy dismantling the monastic system. He promised Henry untold riches and set about delivering them. The suppression of the monasteries was done on the provision that they were corrupt and immoral and had outlived their usefulness. To some extent this was true, but Cromwell's inspectors exaggerated the abuses they found and invented others. First the smaller monasteries were suppressed and their monks and nuns turned out on to the highways. Their contents were appropriated for the royal treasury.

A Victorian engraving showing the trial of Katherine of Aragon.

Then in a second wave of suppressions, all the monasteries were closed. Their magnificent buildings were often demolished and the stones sold off to build new houses for those who were granted or bought their lands; in some cases the lead was stripped from the roofs and they were left to rot. From the aesthetic point of view it was an act of unparalleled national vandalism. Henry did not benefit as much as he might have expected as much of the wealth was redistributed among the new emergent political class from the lower gentry on whose loyalty he now depended, but which had to be bought.

Chapter 6
Bishop John Fisher and
Sir Thomas More

Bishop John Fisher copy after Hans Holbein.

John Fisher, Bishop of Rochester (1469-1535), was born in Beverley, Yorkshire. In 1483 he entered Michael House, Cambridge, where he became a fellow in 1491 and Master in 1497. In 1502 Margaret Beaufort appointed him her Chaplain and Confessor; and in 1503 he persuaded her to endow Cambridge University with a Divinity Chair, to which he was appointed the first Professor. In 1504 he was elected Chancellor of Cambridge University and consecrated Bishop of Rochester.

He was a scholar of international repute. In 1511 he brought Erasmus to Cambridge and they remained lifelong friends. At the age of forty-six he reputedly learnt Greek, and at fifty, Hebrew. He was diligent in his labours towards his diocese and university, and a renowned preacher. In the 1520s he wrote important defences of Catholic theology, including one rebutting Martin Luther's attacks on the King's book, *Assertio Septem Sacramentorum* Defence of the Seven Sacraments - written with the help of Fisher, More and Edward Lee, Archbishop of York. This greatly pleased the King. Fisher became a proponent of the 'New

Learning', which advocated reform of the Catholic Church from within but repudiated Lutheranism.

It all started to go wrong for Fisher when Henry VIII raised the issue of his divorce from Katherine of Aragon. Marital disputes have a tendency to polarise the couples' mutual friends, and the Tudors were no exception. As early as 1526 Fisher had thrown his considerable moral influence against the argument for an annulment, and he totally opposed the break with Rome. He incurred Henry's displeasure when he supported Elizabeth Barton, the Maid of Kent, in her supposedly divine revelations against the divorce; she went to her death in 1534 (see Chapter 8).

In March 1534 he was accused of treason, and in April was sent, along with Sir Thomas More, to the Tower. In May 1535 Pope Paul III made him a cardinal, thinking perhaps Henry would not dare to cut off a cardinal's head. When Cromwell told Henry VIII that the Pope had granted Fisher a Cardinal's hat he reportedly said, *"Yeah, is he so lusty? Well let the Pope send him a hat, but I will so provide that he shall wear it on his shoulders, for head he shall have none to set it on"*. [21]

On 17th June that year Fisher was tried for denial of the King's supremacy. At his trial he steadfastly maintained that, *"Henry, King of England, was not and could never be Supreme Head on Earth of the Church of England"*. On 22nd June he was beheaded on Tower Hill, and went to his death cheerful and courageous. For his execution he wore his finest clothes, saying to his servant, *"Do'st thou not mark that this is our wedding day, and that it behove us to use more cleanliness for solemnity of the marriage?"* He addressed the crowd saying that he was being led to death for wishing to preserve the honour of God. When he was beheaded those present marvelled that so much blood could gush from such an emaciated body, being that of a traitor, was displayed on London Bridge in the usual custom.

Fisher's opposition to the Act of Supremacy had been straightforward and incredibly brave. His opposition was the same as Thomas More's but he made no bones about it, whereas Thomas More argued from a lawyer's point of view, and his main defence was in saying nothing.

Like Sir Thomas More, Fisher was made a saint by Pope Pius XI in 1935; but before we enthuse too much on Fisher's saintliness we should consider the story told in *Foxe's Book of Martyrs*. In 1517 one John Browne was accused of heresy by a priest in Gravesend, with whom he had shared a boat ride. In their conversation Browne had doubted the priest's ability to relieve the sufferings of souls in Purgatory by praying for them. Brown was arrested the following day and sent to Canterbury to be interviewed by Archbishop Wareham and Bishop Fisher.

The prelates ordered that Browne's feet be burnt with hot coals in order to encourage him to deny his heresy, which he would not. Browne later told his story to his wife Elizabeth, when she eventually found him in the stocks at Ashford in Kent. He showed her the soles of his feet, burnt through to the bones, and on which he could no longer stand. Browne was burnt at the stake for heresy the following day. He died with the words, *"Into thy hands I commend my spirit, thou hast redeemed me, O'Lord of truth"*. But truth is often subjective and Fisher could torture and burn someone for holding the wrong version of the truth. At least he had the courage to die for his own version of the truth.

Sir Thomas More was born in 1478 in Milk Street in the City of London, the son of Sir John More, Justice of the Kings Bench. At the age of fifteen the scholarly More was placed in the household of Bishop Morton. Morton was one of the key conspirators who worked with Lady Margaret Beaufort to bring down Richard III and replace him with her son Henry Tudor. Morton reportedly said of the young More to those gathered in his house, *"This child here waiting at table, whosoever shall live to see it, will prove a marvellous man"*. [22]

From there More went to Oxford where he studied Latin and Greek. After leaving Oxford in 1498 he followed his father into the law, entering first New Inn, and then Lincolns Inn. He contemplated becoming a monk but thought better of it and married instead, preferring to be, as he put it, *"A God fearing husband rather than an immoral priest"*.

In the final years of Henry VII's reign he was appointed Under-Sherriff of London and a Member of Parliament. Although there is no documentation to prove it, William Roper's (More's son-in-law) biography of him relates that as an MP he caused serious offence to Henry VII by protesting at the excessive dowry demanded from Parliament for his daughter Margaret's marriage to the King James IV of Scotland. Nevertheless the accession of Henry VIII in 1509 opened up glorious opportunities for gifted men like More with the new golden age of learning and progress promised by the young King.

More established a reputation as an intellectual, a great lawyer, and as a man of principle; such was his reputation that he was invited to join the King's Council in 1517. He held various offices such as Master of Requests (1514), Treasurer of the Exchequer (1521), and Chancellor of the Duchy of Lancaster (1525), and in 1523 he became Speaker of the House of Commons. The King showed him much favour, sending him on diplomatic missions to Francis I and Charles V. The King even paid unexpected visits to his house by the Thames in Chelsea, *"to be merry with him"*. But More had the measure of Henry early on, and as he put it to Roper, *"If my head would win him a castle in France it would not fail to go"*.[23]

More was renowned for being incorruptible and not accepting bribes, something noteworthy at the time; and for his impartiality in judgements of the law. In one case his son-in-law, Giles Heron (see Chapter 13), refused a settlement in a civil case hoping for a more favourable decision in his father-in-law's court; however, he had misjudged More, who found against him. Heron had either not heard, or had not believed, More's famous saying, *"I assure thee on my faith, that if the parties will at my hands call for justice, and, all were it my father stood on the one side and the Devil on the other, his cause being good, the Devil should have the right."*[24] His own father, Judge Sir John More, would no doubt have approved.

More was a courageous man, and witty. In 1523 when Speaker of the House of Commons, Cardinal Wolsey had presented Parliament with a demand to raise £800,000 by means of a 20% tax on all lands and goods in the realm. This was an astronomical amount of money in those times and the House was stunned into silence. Wolsey demanded an answer but no MP would speak. Wolsey turned to More as the Speaker to provide a response. More answered, *"Except that every one of the silent statues around could put into my own head their several wits, I alone am unfit to answer your Grace"*. [25] The Cardinal left in a rage and returned a few days later; only to find that they House asserted its right to hold no debate in his presence. Eventually the amount demanded was reduced, and even that had to be wrung from a reluctant people.

In 1529 More accepted the post of Lord Chancellor, fallen vacant with the dismissal of Wolsey because of his failure to secure the King's divorce. This seems a strange appointment given that More had already made it clear that he thought the King's marriage to Katherine to be valid.

According to More's own account he had obtained the King's liberty to privately dissent on the issue of the divorce before he accepted the post. This is all the odder given that as Lord Chancellor he would have to argue and defend the King's case in Parliament. Perhaps he did not foresee where events were leading, and in any case he could resign if his position became untenable, which is what happened, although not without dire consequences.

In 1532 More, unable to endorse the King's policy on the divorce, resigned the Chancellorship and retired into private life. Henry could not let such a public disapproval of his policy go unaddressed. Henry seems to have genuinely respected and valued More's honesty and integrity, rare qualities in his court, and made various unsuccessful attempts to win him over. But the inevitable confrontation came. More could only look on in horror as the slippery slope to a complete breach with Rome grew steeper. Henry attacked the independent jurisdiction of the church and this culminated in the Act of Supremacy 1534. Not to swear the oath accepting this was treason.

More was arrested and charged and imprisoned in the Tower for a year while Henry hoped he would comply. More would not and he was charged with treason under the Treason Act 1534. The charges are summarised into four counts:

1.   Refusal on 7th May 1535 to accept the Royal Supremacy.

2.   Communication with and support for a known traitor, John Fisher, in his treasonable attitude.

3.   Refusal on 3rd June 1535 to break his silence.

4.   Denial of Parliament's capacity to declare the King the Supreme Head of the Church of England.

On count one More argued that silence in itself was not a crime since it was a principle under English law that silence could be taken as consent. On the second count he contended there was no satisfactory evidence to convict. On the third count he successfully argued that there was no evidence of malicious acts on his part; and that indeed the first three counts were evidence of malicious misrepresentation of his conduct to the King. More was not the foremost lawyer in the land for nothing and won his arguments on these points.

On the fourth and last count he argued that while Parliament might dispose of the crown and hence the succession, it could not dispose of the headship of the Church, as it was a thing spiritual and international. His strongest argument was that the liberty of the Church was guaranteed by Article 1 of Magna Carta, and therefore the King could not infringe it. He said to Thomas Cromwell, his prosecutor who had replaced him as Lord Chancellor, *"And therefore all Christendom is one corps, I can not perceive how any member may without the common assent of the body depart from the common head"*. [26] And with that he sealed his fate. He was found guilty of treason.

Henry spared More the usual horrific commoners' sentence for treason of hanging, drawing and quartering, and commuted it to beheading, the sentence usually reserved for members of the aristocracy. On 7th July 1535 he mounted

Sir Thomas More by Hans Holbein

speech he described himself, *"the King's good servant, but God's first"*. As was the custom with traitors, his head was displayed on Tower Bridge, until some years later when it was blown down in a storm. It was retrieved by his daughter who kept it thereafter. More was declared a Saint by the Catholic Church in 1935.

Henry treated More with a degree of tolerance he did not show to anyone else. He gave him many opportunities to change his position and accept his supremacy. Had he done so he could have enjoyed a quiet life in retirement. But More's genuine religious convictions and the very integrity Henry recognised and valued would now allow him to do so.

More was made a saint by the Catholic Church but we should not forget that for all his admirable qualities and courage he too sent people to their execution for the crime of 'heresy' when he was in office. He was a man of his times and the same strongly held religious convictions and principles that allowed him to go to his own death for his beliefs also allowed him to condemn others for theirs.

the scaffold on Tower Hill, but not without his usual good humour. He said to an attendant, *"Friend help me up; when I come down again I can shift for myself"*. And as he laid his head on the block he asked the axe-man to wait a moment while he put aside his beard, saying, *"For it never committed treason"*. In his short

Chapter 7
Adultery, Incest and Treason: The Boleyn Case

Anne was the daughter of Sir Thomas Boleyn (1477-1539), and Elizabeth Howard, daughter of the Duke of Norfolk. Sir Thomas, was from a prominent Norfolk family and he became an accomplished courtier and diplomat in the service of Henry VII and then Henry VIII. He was rewarded for his services with a peerage as Viscount Rochford in 1525, and then with two Earldoms: as 12th Earl of Wiltshire, and 8th Earl of Ormond in Ireland in 1529 after Anne's rise to favour. He was upwardly mobile and ambitious; being equally ambitious for his family as for himself, grooming his three children, George, Anne and Mary for careers at Court.

His eldest daughter Mary was born, possibly, in 1503 (the exact dates of the births of his children are unknown). Mary was at the French court with her father who was on diplomatic business, along with her younger sister Anne. Here Mary seems to have gained an unfortunate reputation, as years later King Francis I recalled her as *"a hackney"*, or in modern parlance a *'bicycle'*. Fairly or unfairly Mary was noted as *"a very great wanton with a most infamous reputation"*. [27] It is said that Henry first set eyes on both sisters at his meeting with Francis I at the Field of Cloth of Gold in 1520. Mary returned home to marry William Carey, a Gentleman of the Privy Chamber, in 1521, and seems to have soon after become the King's mistress.

Anne, who was born possibly in 1507, was allowed to stay on in the French court. Here she learnt all that was fashionable in terms of dress, manners, dancing, polite conversation and etiquette. This was to serve her in good stead when she returned to England in 1522 where, unlikely as it may seem, all things French were in style. She appeared more French than English, which no doubt gave her an added and exotic appeal. Back home she found a position at Court where her father was now Treasurer of the Household.

Henry and Anne in the spring of 1535 by Victorian artist George Cruikshank.

Anne may not have been conventionally beautiful, but with her long raven black hair, brown eyes, long neck, and strong personality, she was certainly attractive to many. She attracted the attentions of the talented poet Sir Thomas Wyatt, and another suitor, Sir Henry Percy, heir to the Earldom of Northumbria. It seems that Anne would have married Percy but he was promised to another lady; when Percy asked if he could be released from the promise, Cardinal Wolsey got his father the Earl to send him home out of temptation's way; this may be the reason for Anne's intense loathing of Wolsey thereafter.

Mary Boleyn had the good sense not to expect more of Henry than he would freely give; and in any case she was already married. Their affair seems to have ended by 1526 and Henry, turned his attentions to Anne. Love letters between Henry and Anne survive from 1527. Henry wrote to her in French, *"You will expressly certify me of your whole mind concerning the love between us two. For of necessity I must ensure me of this answer, having now above one year struck with the dart of love, not being assured either of failure or of finding a place in your heart and grounded affection. …I will take you for my only mistress, rejecting from thought and affection all others save yourself, to serve you only.*" [28] Anne however had no ambition to be his mistress, only or otherwise; she was playing hard to get, and had no intention of surrendering for anything less than becoming his Queen - quite a strong resolve for a woman of perhaps only twenty years old.

Henry began the long, arduous and ultimately fruitless process of trying to obtain an annulment to his marriage from the Pope. He displayed remarkable and uncharacteristic patience in pursuing Anne. Once he had freed himself from Katherine he could look forward to being the most eligible bachelor in Europe with the pick of the crop; but he pursued Anne with relentless tenacity. Anne, it seems kept Henry at bay for a remarkable six years, until she finally relented and became pregnant in late 1532; they married in January 1533, and she gave birth to Princess Elizabeth in the September.

Anne does not seem to have been a particularly likeable person, nor did she have the diplomatic skills necessary to win the friends and influence the people needed to help her survive in the dangerous position she now occupied. Once ensconced as Queen she had the motto *Ainsi sera, groigne qui groingne* embroidered on her servants coats which means *'This is how it will be, however much people grumble'*, [29] or in modern parlance, 'Like it or lump it'. The common people never liked it, or her, sympathising with Katherine as the wronged wife.

At Anne's coronation in April 1533 many of the Londoners lining the way of the procession from the Tower to Westminster stayed silent and did not doff their hats, while some even shouted *'whore'* as she passed. Her jester shouted back at them, *"I think you have all scurvy heads and dare not uncover"*. They in turn shouted out *"Ha, ha"* in response to the street decorations of 'H.A.' combining the happy couples' initials. [30]

The birth of Princess Elizabeth five months later was a profound and obvious disappointment to Henry, which he could not hide. By now he was also beginning to tire of her nagging ways. Anne could be imperious and arrogant and even spoke to Henry in a way no one else had ever dared. Norfolk remarked that Henry had compared her to Katherine, *"Who never in her life used ill words to him"*. [31] If it was not bad enough to nag her husband she is said to have spoken to her uncle the Duke and, *"used such shameful words to the Duke of Norfolk as one would not address a dog, so that he was compelled to quit the chamber"*. [32] Uncle or no uncle it was a mistake to insult the vindictive Duke. For his part he retaliated by calling her *le grande putain* - the great whore.

With such a home-life even an ordinary mortal might feel the strain. As early as 1534 Henry was discussing the possibility of freeing himself from Anne with his chief advisers Cromwell and Cranmer. Cromwell could see which way the royal wind was blowing and his cunning mind began to turn on devising a plan that would not only free his master but advance his own power and position.

Henry cast his roving eye on a cousin of Anne's, Margaret (Madge) Shelton, governess to Princess Mary, who became his new mistress. Anne reproved him for this but Henry put her in her place by replying that that she had better close her eyes to his unfaithfulness, *"as her betters had done, for he could abase her yet more than he raised her"*. [33] This merely stirred Anne to greater anger. She tried to remove Madge from court but failed, and instead took it out on the Princess Mary whom she abused and described as an *"accursed bastard"*.

The stress was now beginning to tell on Anne, but she placed her hope of safety in producing at least one male heir. Becoming pregnant again in 1535 everything depended on her producing a boy. Instead she miscarried in late January 1536 after hearing the news of Henry's near fatal jousting accident. She was now distracted and panic stricken. And Henry had, had enough. After all, he had fallen in love with another young lady, Jane Seymour.

Henry was convinced that God was still denying him a son and heir and as always looked for someone else to blame. He considered that Anne had, *"seduced him by witchcraft and for that reason considered it* (his marriage) *nul*." [34] Where else should he look for a solution to his problem than to his faithful Cromwell. Henry must have told him to do whatever it took to rid him of Anne for Cromwell would never have dared to embark on the course of action he now followed unless given a free hand by Henry. What followed was the most cynical episode of judicial murder in Henry's entire blood-soaked reign.

Cromwell and Norfolk were instructed to appoint a commission to investigate rumours circulating about Anne at court. At the Mayday tournaments at Greenwich in a chivalrous gesture, Anne dropped her handkerchief to be retrieved by Sir Henry Norris. Henry noticed the gesture, took it as a sign of infidelity, and Cromwell's plan swung into action. Sir Henry Norris was arrested, followed by two gentleman of Henry's privy chamber, Sir Francis Weston and William Brereton. A court musician, Mark Smeaton, was also arrested. And worst of all, her brother, George Boleyn, Lord Rochford, was arrested.

Mark Smeaton, being a mere commoner was tortured on the rack and unsurprisingly confessed to adultery with the Queen. The other four accused denied the accusations. But all to no avail. The charge sheet read that Henry Norris had sex with Anne in the autumn of 1533 after the birth of Princess Elizabeth. William Brereton had sex with her Christmas Day 1533 at Hampton Court. Mark Smeaton and Sir Francis Weston had sex with her at Whitehall. Her own brother Lord Rochford allegedly committed incest with her on 5th November 1535. The dates were all made up by Cromwell, who later admitted as much. Anne was accused of discussing the King's death (treason) with the accused and promised to marry one of them (presumably not her brother) when the King died. [35]

Cromwell managed a show-trial where the jury, made up of peers of the realm, had no doubt of the verdict they were required to reach. The trial began on 12th May and four of the accused, Smeaton, Weston, Brereton and Norris, had already been found guilty of adultery and treason before Anne took the stand on 15th May. She had regained her composure and gave a good account of herself denying the charges. Her brother Lord Rochford also gave a spirited defence but Cromwell's trump card was the 'evidence' of Rochford's own wife Jane, Lady Rochford. Her evidence would have been worthless in any decent court of law. She accused her husband of *"undue familiarity"* with his sister, and that he was, *"always in his sister's room"*: [36] evidence not even worthy of the name 'circumstantial'.

But what followed next would put the jury of Peers in no doubt that a guilty verdict was the only thing that would guarantee their own continued health. Lady Rochford had noted down Anne's remarks about the King's sexual performance: *"The King was not skilful when copulating with a woman and he had not virtue or power"*. [37] The King of the mighty cod-piece was never going to allow such a thing to be said without consequences. The jury of noble peers, including Anne's own uncle the Duke of Norfolk, accordingly found the accused guilty and consigned them all to their fate. The four men were sentenced as traitors to be hung, drawn and quartered. But later Henry graciously commuted this to beheading.

Lord Rochford along with the four others was beheaded on Tower Hill on 17th May. Now that Anne knew her fate her nerves steadied as though a weight had been lifted from her shoulders. She determined to meet her death with dignity. She never admitted her guilt, but was careful not to make passionate declarations of innocence. As with Soviet show-trials the condemned knew that if they did not go quietly it could have severe consequences for their remaining family and friends. Anne could have been burnt at the stake for her 'crimes' but instead a merciful Henry commuted the sentence to beheading, and paid £24 for an expert double-handed swordsman from France.

On the 19th May, the executioner, who knew his job, had hidden his sword under some straw behind him. When Anne mounted the scaffold and laid her head on the block the swordsman called out to someone in the crowd to bring him his sword, Anne lifted up her eyes to see, thereby stretching her neck, and with that he quickly retrieved his sword and took off her head with a single clean blow. She was buried in an old chest used for storing bow staves in the St Peter ad Vincula in the Tower grounds.

Was there anything in the charges? The accused may not have been innocents, but taking liberties with the Queen was a different matter. The atmosphere at court may have been steamy with lots of chivalric exchanges of undying courtly love; but there were known boundaries and everyone knew the fatal consequences of crossing them. There has been speculation that a desperate Anne might have cast around for a lover to impregnate her and pass the child off as the King's. That is possible, but is it likely with five different men, one of whom was her own brother? And in a royal court where life was lived in public and where keeping anything secret for long was well nigh impossible? The jury of history does not believe it even if her jury of peers pretended they did.

Anne had made many enemies at court with her overbearing and haughty manner. She had sympathies with 'new learning' of religious reform, and this earned her the antipathy of the conservative Catholics, such as her uncle the Duke of Norfolk. Henry had grown tired of her and in his egotistical and selfish mind anything she was accused of that allowed him to be rid of her must be true. Cromwell knew his master well and told the Imperial Ambassador Chapuys in an unguarded moment after her execution that he had been, *"authorised and commissioned by the King to prosecute and bring to an end the mistress's trial, to do which he had taken considerable trouble. He had taken, planned and brought about the whole affair".* [38]

Three of those found guilty of adultery with Anne were long-term trusted servants of the King. **Sir Henry Norris** had been one of Henry's closest companions since the early days of his reign. Norris had been the manager of Henry's Privy Chamber from 1526 to

1536; he was a well-liked man known as *"gentle Mr Norris"*; [39] and, *"the best beloved of the King"*.

Sir Francis Weston was a teenager when he joined Henry's circle as a page in 1525, working his way up to being a Gentleman of the Privy Chamber, a most trusted post in which he would sleep outside the King's bedroom ready to respond to his needs at a moment's notice. On Anne's coronation in 1533 Weston was made a Knight of the Bath one of the highest orders of English chivalry. He also was reportedly of a pleasant and respected nature.

Sir William Brereton was likewise a Gentleman of the Chamber with daily access to the King; he was also a land-owner who had made an enemy of Cromwell when he opposed his plans for political reorganisation in Wales. They were all beheaded along with Mark Smeaton on Tower Hill, 17th May 1536.

All three were members of the Boleyn faction at court. Cromwell had been commissioned by Henry to get rid of Anne, but he would have realised that by doing so he would make powerful enemies of her key supporters unless he removed them as well. A simple adulterous affair with the musician Mark Smeaton would have sufficed to get rid of Anne, but Cromwell had to consider a bigger picture. If we assume that none of those accused were actually guilty then Cromwell had removed potential enemies who might seek revenge on her behalf in the future.

Cromwell toyed with implicating others of the Queen's clique but he knew where to draw the line; and he clearly demonstrated his power to bring down even those closest to the King if he put his mind to it. Did Henry really believe that Anne, and his old and trusted companions were guilty of these crimes? Cromwell would never have dared to construct such a case unless he knew he could sell it to Henry. The best that can be said is that he allowed himself to believe Cromwell's lies because it suited him – and Cromwell knew it would. Henry's psychopathic personality could ignore the fate of the innocent pawns involved.

A Victorian view of Anne Boleyn's execution. Note the executioner has a sword, not an axe.

Archbishop Cranmer convened a special court to consider the matter of Anne's relationship with Henry Percy Earl of Northumberland and decided that in their youth a promise of marriage had been made between them and therefore a 'pre-contract' had existed, which meant that Henry and Anne were never legally married in the first place.[40] Cranmer issued an annulment of the marriage. Princess Elizabeth was consequently declared a bastard, to join her already bastardised sister Mary.

Henry happily discovered at the age of forty-five and after two 'marriages' that he had in fact always been a bachelor. No one was impolite enough to mention that if this was the case then Anne and her five co-accused could never have been guilty of adultery or treason in the first place. Some things are best left unsaid.

Henry for his part was relieved and happy. According to the Spanish Ambassador Eustace Chapuys, he happily flaunted Anne's alleged promiscuity, *"He believed more than a hundred had, had to do with her"*. [41] He was vindicated: he had been trapped into an invalid marriage by a wanton witch. He displayed no regrets or conscience about the six lives sacrificed to enable him to marry once again. After a interval of just eleven days Henry married his third wife (or from his point of view his first) Jane Seymour on 30th May.

Chapter 8
Ideological Victims: Martyrs and Heretics

Henry's break with Rome and the Act of Supremacy was radical and revolutionary. Henry replaced the Pope as head of the church in England, but as far as he was concerned both he and the English church remained catholic. It was the Pope who was at fault, not him. Henry continued to adhere to strict catholic doctrine, as evidenced by the *Act Abolishing Diversity in Opinions* (Statute of the Six Articles), or the 'Bloody Statute' of June 1539. Henry had been assiduous in the punishing of heretics before the break with Rome and would continue to be so.

Most people just kept their heads down (in order to keep them on) but others continued their allegiance to the Pope, and had to be punished; and others wanted to go even further and adhere to the new teachings of Martin Luther, and they too had to be punished. Added to that, English translations of the Bible had begun to appear in print and were available to an increasingly literate population. Growing numbers of people were able to make their own interpretations of religious teachings and the first stirrings of freedom of religious thought arose.

Religious dissension and heresy were not new; discontent with the church had stirred as early as the fourteenth century under the Lollards, the followers of John Wyclif. The Lollards were critical of the clergy and challenged some core doctrines, such as Transubstantiation - the belief that the bread used in Holy Communion in the Mass miraculously transforms into Christ's body at the moment of consecration. The Lollards also believed that the best way to purge the church of corruption was to return the clergy to a life of poverty, and it takes little imagination to realise how unpopular that idea was.

Lollards also believed that the Bible should be available to all, and English translations appeared as early as 1390. The Lollard teachings were popular with many but they threatened the established order. They were regarded as heretics and death by burning at the stake was introduced for heresy in 1401; and in 1407 the Lollard translation of the Bible was banned. Lollards were henceforward associated with treason and they were stamped out; although sympathy for their beliefs probably enjoyed continuing underground support up to the Reformation when such beliefs became commonplace.

Henry had broken with Rome in order to secure a divorce and a new wife but he had unintentionally opened up a Pandora's box of religious dissent. William Tyndale (1494-1536) had embarked on the first full-scale English translation of the Bible since the Lollards in the 1520s. His unauthorised version (1535) fulfilled a real need and was popular, indeed it was a milestone in the development of the modern English language; but it drew suspicion and opposition from the authorities. Tyndale fled abroad, but he was executed in 1536 near Brussels by order of the Imperial authorities.

Despite Henry's initial opposition to translations of the Bible he was persuaded by Cromwell that an authorised English version was the best way of containing dissent and retaining ideological control; and one was duly published in 1537, based on the work by Tyndale and Miles Coverdale. A revised Coverdale version was published in 1539 under Cromwell's patronage.

What people believed in was important because the power and legitimacy of the state depended on those beliefs; and for a nation to believe in the wrong things invited the wrath of God. Parallels may be drawn with Communism. In communist ideology no dissent is allowed because it threatens to derail the steady progress of the state to the promised-land of absolute communism: dissent also threatens the power structures of those in control. Those who dissent must be ruthlessly destroyed. So it was in Henry's day.

Unintentional Victims

Elizabeth Barton was a victim of her own making. She was born in 1506 and became known as the Nun, or Maid, of Kent. In 1525 when working as a domestic servant in Aldington in Kent she became ill and fell into a state of religious mania, uttering hysterical ravings. On her recovery she continued to go into trances and make prophesies. She drew so much attention that the Archbishop of Canterbury, William Wareham (c1456-1532), sent two monks to examine her.

One of the monks, **Edward Bocking**, persuaded her that she was directly inspired by the Virgin Mary, while at the same time instructing her in the finer points of theology that differentiated the Catholic Church from the Lutherans. She then became an inmate of the Priory of St Sepulchre, Canterbury, and experienced a lifestyle which must have been an improvement on the drudgery of domestic service.

All went well until the subject of the King's divorce arose. She denounced the divorce, *"in the name and by the authority of God"*, and threatened the King with death if he persisted in his purpose. Archbishop Wareham was convinced of her genuineness and even Wolsey granted her an audience. Sir Thomas More also met with her, and Bishop Fisher wept with joy over her revelations.

Henry's divorce and marriage to Anne Boleyn in 1533, and his subsequent failure to die, took the wind of our Elizabeth's prophetical sails. Meanwhile her protector Wareham had died and More and Fisher were themselves in serious trouble because of their opposition to Henry's investiture of himself as the head of the English church.

Barton was interrogated and in September 1533 made a full confession that she, *"never had visions in all her life, but all that she ever said was feigned of her own imagination only, to satisfy the minds of those which resorted to her, and to obtain worldly praise"*. After being made to publicly recant she was imprisoned and tried for high treason. She was found guilty and executed at

Tyburn, along with Bocking and four other accomplices, on 20th April 1534. In her final words she described herself thus, *"a poor wench without learning, who had been puffed up by praise to her own undoing and that of her companions"*. [42]

Martyrs

The Carthusians were stricter followers of the Benedictine monastic lifestyle and were widely respected for the integrity and the sanctity of their lives. Henry was therefore keen to win them over to his point of view. However under the leadership of their Prior **John Houghton** (1488-1535) they refused to swear to the Act of Supremacy; thereby earning Henry's especial vindictiveness. Houghton was tried for treason and said that he, *"cannot take the King, our Sovereign Lord to be Supreme Head of the Church of England afore the apostles of Christ's Church"*. Houghton was standing by the doctrine of Apostolic Succession whereby all Popes claim the right to represent the Church on earth according to Christ's handing of the responsibility to St Peter, the first Bishop of Rome, of which they are the heirs. John Houghton was found guilty of treason and hung drawn and quartered at Tyburn, (now Marble Arch) on 4th May 1535.

Houghton was executed wearing his monk's habit on Henry's orders as a warning and example to others. Houghton was accompanied on the day by two other priors from other monasteries who also refused to swear to the Act of Supremacy: **Robert Lawrence**, Prior of the Carthusian monastery at Beauvale in Nottinghamshire, and **Augustine Webster**, Prior of the Carthusian monastery at Axholme in Lincolnshire.

Further executions of Carthusian monks followed for the same offence. **William Exemere**, **Humphrey Middlemore** and **Sebastian Newdigate** of the Charterhouse were executed on 19th June 1535, at Stepney, East London, then just outside the City boundaries. Newdigate had been a Gentleman of Henry's Privy Chamber and a friend of the King, but had resigned his position and left the court over the issue of the

King's divorce. Executed along with them were **Richard Reynolds** of Syon Abbey, and **John Haile** a priest,

The Carthusian monks remained intransigent and more executions followed. **John Rochester** and **James Walworth** from the Charterhouse of St Michael in Hull, Yorkshire, were arrested for treason and condemned to death on 11th May 1537. They were hung in chains from the battlements of the city of York until dead.

Henry now became even more enraged. On 18th May 1537 the twenty monks and eighteen lay brothers remaining in the London Charterhouse were required to swear to the Act of Supremacy. Of these, four of the monks refused: **Thomas Johnson**, **Richard Bere**, **Thomas Green**, and **John Davey**. Six of the lay brothers also refused: **Robert Salt**, **William Greenwood**, **Thomas Redyng**, **Thomas Scrynen**, **Walter Pierson**, and **William Horne**. All the rest capitulated, took the oath, and were then expelled from the Charterhouse to roam abroad.

The ten remaining intransigents were taken to Newgate Prison where they were left standing, chained to the wall with their hands behind them, and left to starve to death. However, **Margaret Clements** (nee Giggs), a lady who had been raised in the household of Thomas More, bribed the jailor to let her visit them and she smuggled in some food. When the jailor found out he feared for his own safety and the visits were stopped. Seven of them died of starvation between 6th to 16th June. It is possible that at this point Cromwell ordered the three survivors to be fed so that they could be tried and executed; however two of the remaining died later, Richard Bere on 9th August, and Thomas Johnson on 20th September.

William Horne was kept alive and not condemned to death for another three years. Horne was finally hanged, drawn and quartered at Tyburn on 4th August 1540. He died in company of five others: **Robert Bird**, **Giles Heron**, Friar **Lawrence Cook**, Prior of Doncaster, and a priest, **William Bird**.

Heretics

Next we come to the executions for heresy, for which the punishment was burning at the stake. **John Forrest** (1471-1538) had studied at Oxford to become a Doctor of Divinity and had risen to be the head of the Franciscan monks in England, and Confessor to Katherine of Aragon. Among Forrest's heretical beliefs was that the Catholic Church was the Church of Rome; that Englishmen should believe in the Pope's power to forgive sins; and that the intercession of priests could reduce the time truly repentant sinners spent in Purgatory.   Forrest at first swore to the Act of Supremacy but then claimed that this had been an oath, *"taken by his outward man, but the inward man never consented"*. [43] Given the chance to swear yet again he proudly refused and said that he rejected it as 'the work of the devil'.

Found guilty of heresy, on 22nd May 1538 he was dragged on a hurdle from Newgate prison to Smithfield to be burnt outside the church of St Bartholomew the Great. Many of the Great and Good were there to see the spectacle along with thousands of Londoners. The victim was subjected to the preliminary torture of having to listen to a three-hour sanctimonious sermon delivered by Bishop Stephen Gardiner. He was then hauled up by chains around his body to dangle as a bonfire was lit beneath him. He took two hours to die as his legs and lower body was consumed by the flames; he finally gave out when the flames reached his chest.

With penalties like those on offer only the most intransigent would resist. One such was **John Lambert,** also known as **John Nicholson.** Lambert endured the bizarre experience of being tried in the presence of Henry VIII himself. Lambert was a former chaplain and schoolmaster who had already been found guilty of heresy in a trial by Archbishop Cranmer, but Henry wished to question him personally.

Henry entered the court dressed entirely in white satin (to symbolise his purity no doubt). He demanded to know if Lambert accepted that the Eucharist (communion bread on consecration) was the body of Christ?   Lambert equivocated, and when Henry demanded a yes or no answer he replied, *"It is not His body, I deny it"*. Henry declared the verdict, *"Mark well, for now you shall be condemned even by Christ's own words, "This is my body"*. [44] Lambert was burnt in the same manner as John Forrest, on 22nd November 1538 at Smithfield. The bonfire had consumed his legs but the fire was dying down and Lambert was still alive. So the executioners hoisted him off the chains with their pikes and dropped him into the fire.

Robert Barnes (1495-1540) was a former Augustinian monk who had been a friend of Cromwell's and had been sent to Germany to help negotiate the terms of Henry's marriage to Anne of Cleves. In February 1540 Barnes had preached a sermon critical of Stephen Gardiner, Bishop of Winchester and orthodox doctrines. He, along with two of his fellow dissenters, **William Jerome**, Vicar of Stepney, and **Thomas Garret**, were summoned to Henry's presence at Hampton Court. They recanted of their views to the King who then dismissed them. The vindictive Bishop Gardiner however had them arrested and imprisoned in the Tower. They withdrew their earlier recantation to the King and stood by their views. All three were found guilty of heresy and burnt on 30th July 1540.

Barnes had been close to Cromwell and his reformist religious views. By picking Barnes off Gardiner and the religious conservatives were incriminating Cromwell by association and signalling that he would be the next victim, which indeed he was, not long afterwards. Many others suffered the fate of martyrdom for their religious views, either for holding to the old traditional doctrines or espousing new ones, both were considered heretical unless they suited the King's view of what was allowed, or not, to be believed.

Anne Askew 1546

Anne Askew was one of the final ideological victims. She born near Grimsby in Lincolnshire in 1521 of the minor gentry; she was a convert to the Reformers of the Protestant cause and, accordingly, disowned and turned out of the house by her staunchly Roman Catholic husband. Undaunted she would read the Bible from the aisles of Lincoln cathedral to any who would listen. She went to London in 1545 to sue for a separation from her husband. Her views being known, she was arrested, charged with heresy, and sent to Newgate prison. She was then examined by the Bishop of London and others on the doctrine of transubstantiation, or 'the real presence' which she refuted.

She was summoned to the Privy Council in Greenwich and they did their best to persuade her to recant her ideas. She refused and was sent to the Tower. Sir Richard Rich and Thomas Wriothesley caused her to be racked and attempted to get her to incriminate members of Henry's court. Even after two sessions of torture she would not do so and the Lieutenant of the Tower refused to torture her again, whereupon Rich and Wriothesley tortured her themselves. Still she refused to recant or incriminate others.

She was put on trial in the Guildhall. In the full knowledge that her intransigence would earn her the death sentence, she said to the Court, *"That which you call God is a piece of bread; for proof thereof let it lie in a box three months and it will be mouldy. I am persuaded it cannot be God".* The Court was equally persuaded that she was a heretic and, along with three others, she was condemned to die. The rack had destroyed her limbs and she had to be carried to the place of execution in a chair. She was burnt sitting down, in front of St Bartholomew's Church on in Smithfield on 16th July 1546.

Chapter 9
Casualties of the Suppression of the Monasteries

It isn't possible here to list all those who lost their lives resisting the suppression of the monasteries but here are just a few.

Adam Sedbar had been appointed abbot of the Cistercian abbey Jervaulx in Wensleydale, Yorkshire in 1533. He reluctantly joined the Pilgrimage of Grace as a protest at the King's dissolution of the monasteries, but the peaceful protest degenerated into violence, as mass protests often do. The King's measures to suppress it caused Sedbar, along with others, to seek sanctuary with John Scrope, 8th Baron Scrope of Bolton, in Bolton Castle. The enclosing forces of the King forced Scrope to flee for his life, and Sedbar hid out on Witton Fell for a few days but was captured on 12th May 1537 and taken to London.

Sedbar was imprisoned in the Beauchamp Tower in the Tower of London, where he inscribed his name which can still be seen, *"ADAM SEDBAR. ABBAS JOREVALL 1537. His charge sheet read, "He did conspire to deprive the King of his title of Supreme Head of the English Church, and to compel him to hold a certain Parliament and convocation of the clergy of the realm, and did commit divers insurrections."* He was tried on 24th May and was found guilty, along with a number of others. He was executed on 2nd June 1537 at Tyburn by hanging, drawing and quartering. He was executed along with the Prior of Bridlington Abbey, and their heads were displayed on London Bridge, along with those of two others executed a few days before, the Abbot of Fountains Abbey, and the Prior of Gainsborough Abbey.

Richard Whiting (1461-1539) had a long and distinguished career in the Church, being appointed the Abbot of Glastonbury, by Cardinal Wolsey in 1525; and according to contemporary accounts he was conscientious and well respected. Glastonbury Abbey was one of the richest in the land and housed about a hundred monks. Whiting had signed the Act of Supremacy in 1534 and was not therefore in opposition to the King. But Glastonbury was a rich prize and Cromwell sent the Royal Commissioners in to examine Whiting and the Abbey's affairs. Some small faults were found, and the Abbot's jurisdiction over the town of Glastonbury was removed. When the Suppression of the Religious Houses Act (1535) brought about the dissolution of the lesser monasteries, Whiting was assured that Glastonbury was safe.

By 1539 Glastonbury was the only abbey left in Somerset. Cromwell sent the Royal Commissioners in again to find fault and close the abbey. Whiting refused to surrender the Abbey as it did not fall under the jurisdiction of the 1535 Act. Whiting was arrested along with two others and sent to the Tower. Cromwell manufactured charges against them, the details of which are unknown, but involved treason and the alleged stealing of Abbey funds.

The ruins of Tintern Abbey in the Wye Valley, just one of hundreds of monastic victims of Henry.

The treason charges were most likely the alleged finding of written arguments by Whiting, *"on behalf of Queen Katherine"*. [45] As a member of the House of Lords, Whiting had the right to be tried by Parliament and sentenced by Act of Attainder; but such was Cromwell's cynical disregard for the law he was sent back to Glastonbury for trial with his two companions. They were found guilty and sentenced to death. Whiting, now aged about 78, was, along with the monks, John Thorne and Roger James, hung drawn and quartered. Whiting's head was displayed over the West Gate of the empty abbey and his four quarters were displayed at Wells, Bath, Ilchester and Bridgewater.

The Pilgrimage of Grace began as a religious protest, but Henry treated it as armed rebellion.

Hugh Cook Faringdon, born Cook, he adopted the name of Faringdon sometime prior to 1500 and became a monk in Reading Abbey. He was elected Abbot in 1520; he also served as a Justice of the Peace, and in various local government positions. He was the King's host in 1521 and he became a Royal Chaplain. He was an MP from 1523 to 1539 and was supportive of the King's quest for a divorce. In 1536 he signed the Articles of Faith which virtually acknowledged the royal supremacy of Crown over Church. He sang the requiem mass for Queen Jane Seymour in 1537. Cook even seems to have co-operated with the Commissioners sent to suppress Reading Abbey.

But in 1539 he was indicted for Treason, being accused of assisting the Northern rebels with money. As a mitred abbot he was entitled to be tried by Parliament, but Cromwell had decided the verdict before the trial began. Faringdon was found guilty and hung, drawn and quartered before the Abbey Gatehouse on 14th November 1539 along with two co-accused, **John Rugge**, and **John Eynon**, the Priest of St Giles Church, Reading.

These are just a few of the deaths that accompanied the suppressions of the monasteries that led to the next great blood-letting – the rebellion of the Pilgrimage of Grace.

Chapter 10
Rebellion: The Pilgrimage of Grace

The dissolution of the monasteries and the overturning of a centuries old social order caused widespread discontent, especially in the north of England. The monasteries used to look after the poor, destitute and dying, and provide employment to many. Thomas Cromwell acknowledged this gap in the social fabric by passing the **Beggars Act** of 1536. This required the local parish or municipalities to assume responsibility for the "impotent poor". [46] Those capable of work were given it or taught a trade; "sturdy beggars" were to be punished. But these measures did not assuage the discontent, especially not where they were caused by genuine religious conviction. A few monasteries resisted closure by the threat of force of arms but these mini-rebellions were soon put down.

In September 1536 more dangerous resistance broke out in Lincolnshire. The uprising spread across the north of England to Yorkshire. The rebels demanded to keep the old religion, the restoration of the monasteries, less taxation, and Cromwell's life. They went so far as to kill two of the King's commissioners. This rebellion was not just one of the common people but included members of the minor aristocracy, who would normally be relied on to support the King and suppress discontent. Such a rising represented a real and dangerous threat to the regime.

By October the rebels had entered the city of Lincoln and their numbers had grown into thousands. Henry was incandescent with rage and had cause for serious alarm. He sought to pacify the rebels by denying further taxes were planned, yet demanded they surrender one hundred of their ringleaders. But his threats of destruction to them and their families were for the moment empty as he had no way of enforcing them.

The King appointed the Duke of Norfolk to crush the rebellion. Norfolk was his most experienced general, but there was no standing army and it took time to raise and equip soldiers, and he lacked money to pay for them. The rebel numbers were now thought to be in the region of 40,000 to 50,000, and hundreds more joined them by the day. The city of York was captured by the rebels and the revolt spread across the northern counties. They now styled themselves the **Pilgrimage of Grace** and marched with banners embroidered with the five wounds of Christ, His sacred monogram of IHS and an image of a chalice. [47] Their leader was one **Robert Aske**.

Little is known of Robert Aske but that he was a one-eyed London lawyer in his thirties who had formerly been a servant of Henry Percy, 6th Earl of Nothumberland. [48] Aske met with the King's messenger but refused to allow him to read out the King's message to the rebels. Aske instead said that he would lead his pilgrimage to London to see the King, and there he would, *"have all the vile blood put from his council and noble blood set up again; to have the faith of Christ and God's laws kept and restitution done for wrongs done to the Church"*. [49] The luckless herald, **Thomas Mylner,** fell to his knees and begged to be allowed to read the royal proclamation. Refusing again, Aske sent him on his way.

Norfolk did not yet have sufficient forces to crush the rebellion and what he had were hampered by bad weather. Henry now had to dissemble and invited Aske to London to submit his grievances. The King's latest wife, Jane Seymour is thought to have pleaded with Henry on her knees to restore the lesser monasteries, the dissolution of which had provoked the rebellion. Henry reportedly told her to mind her own business and remember the fate of her predecessor.[50]

Henry understood the danger to his crown if the rebellion spread further and so he welcomed Aske to his court and turned on all his old charm. He listened to Aske and gave him his personal assurances that there would be redress for the rebels' grievances. He presented him with a new crimson silk jacket and sent him back to Doncaster with the promise of a pardon, and that he would ride north himself to direct operations. A general pardon was offered to the Yorkshire rebels and a conference was promised to consider their proposals. They dispersed, while Norfolk was busy rounding up and interrogating the Lincolnshire rebels.

Aske naively believed that the King was led astray by evil advisors like Cromwell, and Henry was happy to let him believe it. The rebels 24 Articles were presented to Norfolk in 6th December 1536 and it was agreed that if the rebels disbanded: the King would receive their demands; Parliament would discuss them; and all the 'pilgrims' would be pardoned for their rebellion. This bought Henry valuable time, and many of pilgrims took the opportunity to now return to their homes.

In January 1537 fresh rebellions broke out in Yorkshire when it was realised that Henry was making preparations to subdue the county. The leaders this time were **John Hallam** who had been prominent in the Pilgrimage of Grace and **Sir Francis Bigod**. But they had misjudged the public appetite for further rebellion and the risings were quickly subdued by Norfolk. The King wrote to Norfolk, *"You must cause such dreadful execution upon a good number of the inhabitants, hanging them on trees, quartering them and setting their heads and quarters in every town as shall be a fearful warning"*. [51] Martial law was imposed and normal jury trials dispensed with. A reported **216** persons were executed - which given the tens of thousands who participated in the rebellions might in Henry's terms be seen as the North getting off lightly.

Aske had helped in the subduing of rebellion in Scarborough and Hull in early 1537 but Cromwell used the excuse of a letter from him to **Lord Darcy** to arrest him for treason and imprison him in the Tower. Thomas Darcy (1467-1537) (1st Baron Darcy of Darcy or Templehurst) had been a faithful servant of Henry VII and Henry VIII but had joined the Pilgrimage of Grace. Darcy was interrogated in the Tower, and with nothing to lose told Cromwell, *"It is you that are the very original and chief cause of all this rebellion and mischief. Though you would procure all the noblemens' heads within this realm to be struck off, yet shall one head remain, that shall strike off your head"*. [52] If he meant Henry he was to be proved right.

Aske was condemned, taken to York and hanged. Darcy was beheaded at Tower Hill. Another notable person, **John Lord Hussey**, Butler of England, a former chamberlain to Princess Mary was also implicated and he was executed in Lincoln. **Sir Francis Bigod** and **John Hallam** were also executed.

Thomas Mylner, who had failed to deliver Henry's message to Aske at York, was found guilty of treason and executed for the crime of kneeling to Aske and begging him to hear the King's message.

Chapter 11

More Nobility Destroyed 1537–1541: the Poles, Courtneys, and Nevilles

*A*s Henry grew older and his health declined, and the survival of his dynasty depended on his only son the young Edward, so the perceived threat of the surviving heirs of the Yorkist royal family grew greater in his mind; as no doubt it grew in the mind of Thomas Cromwell, whose own survival depended on that of the Tudor dynasty. The Pole family were tainted by the treasonous activities of their relative, Cardinal Reginald Pole, and this was made worse by Henry's inability to lay his hands on the Cardinal himself. The Poles were descended from George Duke of Clarence, through his daughter Margaret who married Sir Richard Pole.

Cromwell in true KGB style moved against the weakest member of the Pole family first in order to use him to incriminate the rest; and he had planted his own spies in the Pole households. On 29th August 1538 he arrested **Sir Geoffrey Pole**, the younger brother of the Cardinal, with whom he was accused of having treasonous correspondence. In the intimidating environment of the Tower of London his spirit was quickly broken and he agreed to turn King's evidence against his family. Then, as they say, sang like a canary.

Sir Geoffrey revealed that his brother **Henry Pole 1st Baron Montague** had said, *"I like well the proceedings of my brother the Cardinal…but I like not the doings in this realm, and I trust to see a change of this world. I would that we were both over the sea. The world in England waxes all crooked; God's law is turned upside down, abbeys and churches overthrown. I think they will cast down the parish churches."* Then he is supposed to have dreamed that the King were dead and said, *"The King is not dead but he will die one day suddenly, his leg will kill him and we shall have jolly stirring"*.[53] All of this was treason; and expressed what many people were thinking.

In November 1538 Cromwell moved against the rest. He arrested **Margaret Countess** of Salisbury (Cardinal Pole's mother), **Henry Pole 1st Baron Montague**, **Henry Courtney Marquis of Exeter** and his wife **Gertrude**, **Sir Edward Neville**, and **Lord Delawarr**. Even the young sons of Henry Pole and Henry Courtney were arrested even though they were minors, twelve and fourteen years old. The drearily predictable trials were held on 2nd December that year. Montague was tried in Westminster Hall in front of a jury of Peers. The charges were that he, *"devised to maintain, promote and advance one Reginald Pole (the Cardinal) …enemy to the King beyond the seas and to deprive the King of his throne".* [54] The verdict was guilty. The rest were tried the following day and found guilty of treason.

Henry Courtney, Marquis of Exeter, was descended from King Edward IV through his daughter Catherine. He had benefited in the early days of Henry's reign when the Pole, Courtney and Neville families had been restored to favour. Henry Courtney had been a member of the King's council in the early days. The Poles and the Courtney's were religious conservatives and Cromwell had a vested interest in destroying them since he promoted the 'new learning'. If and when Henry died, had the conservatives regained power (as they did), then his days would be numbered, luckily for him by that time he was already dead.

Sir Edward Neville had been knighted by the King at the siege of Tournai in 1513 and had risen to become Standard Bearer and Master of the Buckhounds. He hated Cromwell and the religious reforms. He had unwisely expressed the view that, *"The King keeps knaves and fools here that we dare neither look nor speak, and if I were able, I would rather live any life in the world than tarry in the privy chamber."* He equally unwisely expressed his view about Cromwell when he said, *"I trust knaves* (Cromwell) *shall he put down and lords reign, and that the world will amend one day"*. And surely the remark that would have sealed his fate in any circumstances was that he had reportedly said, *"The King is a beast, and worse than a beast."* [55]

Thomas Lord Delawarr, was not a prime mover in the conspiracy, such as it was, and he managed to secure his pardon by relinquishing his estates to the King. The hapless **Geoffrey Pole** was granted a full pardon in January 1539 for turning King's evidence. He made an unsuccessful suicide attempt while in the Tower, and roamed Europe on his release; finally dying in 1558, in what state of mind we can only guess.

Sir Edward Neville was beheaded on Tower Green on 8th December 1538, and a number of commoners implicated in the treason were hung, drawn and quartered. **Henry Pole** and **Henry Courtney** were beheaded on Tower Green on 9th January The Marchioness of Exeter and Lady Courtney were pardoned. Margaret Pole, Countess of Salisbury, had to wait longer to meet her fate.

Edward Courtney.

Although only twelve years old at the time, Edward was arrested with his father, Henry Courtney, and imprisoned in the Tower. His father was Henry VIII's cousin, his mother having been the sister of Henry's mother Elizabeth of York. The King seems to have been slightly less vindictive towards him than Henry Pole the younger. Edward was allowed some tuition and reasonably decent living conditions. Nevertheless he was kept imprisoned for fifteen years and only released on the accession of Mary I in 1553.

Henry Pole, the younger

Henry Pole, son of the 1st Baron Montague, had played no part in his father's treasonable activities, being just a boy of fourteen. Nevertheless, Henry consigned him to imprisonment in the Tower. Henry now hated the Pole family with a vengeance. He executed the aged Margaret Pole Countess of Salisbury in 1541: but what to do about young Henry? He might have followed his grandmother Margaret to the block in 1541 but he was still a minor and perhaps even Henry VIII baulked at the idea, and the public relations disaster, of executing an underage boy on the basis of no evidence whatsoever.

Instead he ordered that the boy be imprisoned in solitary confinement. He was refused a tutor or any kind of education or stimulation. The King ordered that he was to be *"poorly and strictly kept, and not desired to know anything"*. A record of 1542 shows payment for his food, but after that there is nothing and we must assume that he died sometime during Henry's reign.

Some have speculated that he was starved to death; or that when he had passed from the public's mind a more direct method of dispatching him was used. In any case he died alone and forgotten in the Tower. This staggering cruelty and callousness towards a young boy is hard to comprehend. But after the way Henry had destroyed the boy's family he posed a threat not only to Henry but to his heir Edward. Henry VIII was following the precedent set by his father and the cruel years of imprisonment and eventual execution of the young Edward Plantagenet in 1499.

Margaret Pole, Countess of Salisbury

Margaret Pole's judicial murder by Henry VIII was hardly even that since any genuine legal process was almost entirely dispensed with. Her death is one of the most unjust and inhuman that Henry VIII was responsible for.

Margaret Plantagenet was born in August 1473 in Castle Farley near Bath. She was the daughter of George Duke of Clarence, and his wife Isabel, daughter of Richard Neville Earl of Warwick, the 'Kingmaker'. Her mother died in 1477 of 'childbed fever', and her father was executed for treason in 1478 by his brother Edward IV. She was brought up in the Queen's household along with the Princesses. Her lineage was Plantagenet on both sides, but her father's crime of treason and his Attainder, meant her brother, Edward Earl of Warwick could not inherit the throne.

In 1485 the eight year old Margaret came under the control of the new King, Henry VII. He later married her off to the safe keeping of Sir Richard Pole in 1491 when she was seventeen, the groom being about twenty years older.

The arms of Margaret, Countess of Salisbury. The arms of England in top left hand quarter show how dangerously close to the throne her ancestry was.

Sir Richard was a Knight of the Garter and a squire of Henry's bodyguard. Margaret and Richard had four sons: Henry, Arthur, Reginald, Geoffrey, and a daughter Ursula. Sir Richard Pole was a loyal and active supporter of the Tudor monarch, and by the end of the century he had been appointed as Chief Gentleman of the Privy Chamber to Prince Arthur, Henry VII's eldest son and heir. Sir Richard resided in Wales with the young Prince and headed-up the local government on the King's behalf. Sir Richard died in 1505

Margaret's brother Edward, Earl of Warwick, was judicially murdered on trumped up charges in 1499 after nearly a lifetime's imprisonment in the Tower. Perhaps to make amends and reward her loyalty, on his accession Henry VIII granted the young widow, his *"good cousin"*, an annuity of £100. In 1513 he again showed his favour when he bestowed on her the title of Countess of Salisbury, and reversed the Attainder on her murdered brother, thereby restoring the rights of the family. Margaret was in royal favour and became a firm friend of Katherine of Aragon. Of her sons, the eldest son Henry was created 1st Baron Montague; Arthur was knighted and created a Gentleman of the Privy Chamber; Reginald was academically minded and educated for the church; and Geoffrey was also knighted. Ursula was married to Henry Stafford, heir to the Duke of Buckingham.

Through her friendship with Queen Katherine, Margaret was appointed to the post of Lady Mistress of Princess Mary's household. The family basked in the sun of Henry's favour and all looked well. In 1521 the execution of the Duke of Buckingham put the family under a cloud; but Margaret remained at court however, and in 1525 accompanied Princess Mary to Wales. But by 1526 Henry had decided to rid himself of his wife and Margaret's loyalty would be tested and found wanting. One was either with Henry or against him – and even being with him wasn't always particularly safe.

Margaret refused to abandon her friendship and loyalty to Katherine. She was particularly attached to Princess Mary, who regarded her as a second mother. The long story of the divorce progressed and in 1533 after his marriage to Anne Boleyn,

Margaret refused to surrender Princess Mary's jewels to the new Queen. She was dismissed from her post as governess to the Princess, although she offered to stay with Mary at her own expense, Henry made sure that they were parted.

After Anne Boleyn's fall in 1536, Margaret was restored to a position at court, but now a fresh storm threatened her safety. Her son, Cardinal Reginald Pole had written a book attacking Henry's divorce from Katherine and his assumption of head of the English church. Henry had been Reginald's patron in his studies and he was furious with his disloyalty. Reginald, and all the Pole family, now became the subjects of Henry's hatred and paranoia. Henry forced Margaret to write letters denouncing Reginald as a traitor and regretting giving birth to him, which were then sent to Reginald in Rome.

The family were now subjects of Henry's deepest suspicions. The religious and social revolution that he had begun, engineered by Cromwell, now made him vulnerable to rebellion; as was indeed the case in 1537. Henry privately told the French ambassador that he intended to *"destroy them all"*. And the man to do the job was Cromwell. Cromwell had planted spies in her household to gather, or manufacture, evidence against her and her sons. In August 1538 they were arrested, as narrated above.

Margaret was held and interrogated in her own house at Warblington in Hampshire. She kept her nerve and did not incriminate herself despite long hours of questioning. They seized letters, and a tunic of white silk embroidered with the Arms of England, on the back of which was sewn the badge of the Five Wounds of Christ, the emblem of the rebels of the Pilgrimage of Grace. Whether this was genuine or planted who can say, but it was sufficient 'evidence' to condemn her. Margaret was taken to Cowdray House, the home of William Fitzwilliam, Earl of Southampton. She remained there a prisoner until March 1539 when she was taken to the Tower of London.

Cromwell moved a Bill of Attainder against her in Parliament, without a full trial; dispensing with a trial was a legal refinement of Cromwell's to save time, trouble and uncertainty of outcome. The evidence against her included the incriminating garment, as well as treasonous correspondence with her son the Cardinal. The Bill was passed on 12th May 1539, but the penalty of death was not enacted immediately. It was even thought that she might be pardoned and released, but instead she languished in the Tower. Henry's fifth wife Catherine Howard even got into trouble for sending her warm nightwear for the draughty conditions.

Perhaps even Henry hesitated to execute an ageing and frail lady, and so kept her imprisoned in the Tower for the next two years. But in April 1541 his mind was made up for him. Another rebellion was threatened in the north of England. Henry decided to act despite the fact that Margaret posed no direct threat. Early in the morning of 27th May 1541, Margaret was told that she would be executed within the hour. It was usual to allow the condemned a day or two to put their affairs in order and to prepare themselves. The execution took place in front of the Lord Mayor of London and a select group of dignitaries.

There is no authoritative account of what actually happened on Tower Green that morning but two versions survive. Both agree that the executioner was incompetent. According the Calendar of State Papers, he was described as, *"a wretched and blundering youth…who literally hacked her head and shoulders to pieces in the most pitiful manner"*. In one version of the story the sixty seven year old lady was defiant, and said she was *"guilty of no crime"*, refusing to kneel and put her head on the block. The other version is that she was distracted, or perhaps by now senile, and did not realise what was happening, and so set off to wander aimlessly around Tower Green.

Both versions agree that the executioner brought her to the block but missed with his first blow, instead dealing her a glancing blow on the shoulder, which set her off running.

He then dragged her back to the block and is said to have hacked her to death, dealing up to eleven strokes before successfully taking off her head.

Margaret was buried like many similar noble victims in the Chapel of St Peter ad Vincula (St Peter in Chains) in the Tower of London. The Tower of London is said to be one of the most haunted places in England, and one of the most harrowing ghost stories is that on the anniversary of her execution Margaret comes back to re-enact the horrific events of that May morning.

Chapter 12
More Treason: 1537-1539

Irish politics is a quagmire of violence right up to the present day. Ireland had been invaded and settled by the Vikings, just as England had. England first became embroiled in Ireland when Richard de Clare, Earl of Pembroke, nicknamed Strongbow, invaded with a small force in 1169 during the reign of Henry II. Norman involvement continued for the simple reason that Ireland represented a back door for invasion to England by a foreign power, just as Scotland did. English Monarchs had to look on both nations as potential hosts to foreign foes. The Norman, and later the English, solution in Ireland was to subdue and control it as far as possible.

By Henry VIII's time the English portion of the population followed the Reformation, while the Irish population held to the supremacy of the Pope. Cardinal Wolsey had appointed Archbishop John Alan to the See of Dublin from 1528-1536, and he dissolved forty of the smaller monasteries. In 1537 a Parliament assembled in Dublin to enact the Act of Supremacy. Henry had toyed with the idea of making his illegitimate son Henry Fitzroy King of Ireland but the boy died aged 17 in 1536. Henry declared himself King of Ireland, his previous title merely being Lord of Ireland.

Thomas Fitzgerald, 10th Earl of Kildare, one of the principal lords in Ireland, rebelled in 1534. He had become angry at the measures taken to curb his family's power and the promoting of his rivals. He began the Kildare Rebellion and appealed to Charles V the Holy Roman Emperor and the Pope for support. The rebellion was a unsuccessful and he surrendered to Lord Leonard Grey in 1535. He had been promised a pardon, but was betrayed and was executed as a traitor along with five of his uncles.

Lord Leonard Grey (1490-1541), 1st Viscount Grane, had been appointed Marshall of the English Forces in 1534, and appointed Lord Deputy in 1535. Grey was proud, haughty and quarrelsome but he successfully fulfilled his commission to put down the rebellion of those opposed to the Act of Supremacy. He was created Viscount Grane, 2nd January 1536. However, he fell foul of a problem that bedevilled future deputies in Ireland: if he was too hard on the rebels he stoked up further rebellion, but if he attempted conciliatory policies he was mistrusted by the powers at home.

Grey did follow a policy of conciliation towards the Irish religious conservatives and was called back home in 1540. He was accused of allowing his nephew the young Earl of Kildare to escape to France in 1539. He denied the accusation and threw himself on the mercy of the King, but nevertheless was found guilty of treason and beheaded on Tower Hill 28th July 1541.

Sir Nicholas Carew (1496-1539) was another of those curious cases of a close and trusted companion of Henry VIII whom he nevertheless later turned against and executed. Carew was a fearless jouster,

a man after Henry's own heart and numbered among his favourites. He was a Groom of the Privy Chamber in 1511, and was knighted around 1517.

Sir Nicholas Carew by Hans Holbein.

He held a number of prominent offices, including, Master of the Horse, Master of the Forests, and Lieutenant of Ruysbank – responsibility for guarding Calais harbour. His appointment to

Calais in 1519, away from the court, was reputedly to teach him a lesson because he had become over familiar with the King, 'not regarding his estate or degree'.

He was also entrusted with important diplomatic missions; to France in 1521; and again to France in 1524, to represent the English at the peace talks between Francis I and Charles V, the Holy Roman Emperor. He could undertake responsible roles but Cardinal Wolsey saw him as too influential and engineered his removal from the King's Privy Chamber in 1526; however in 1528 he was restored to that position, possibly because of the influence of Anne Boleyn, his distant relative.

Carew eventually fell out with Anne, probably because of his loyalty to Queen Katherine, and his disapproval of her conduct. He was said to sympathise with Princess Mary, whom Anne treated badly. Carew aligned himself with Cromwell and the religious conservatives who both wanted Anne Boleyn gone. In 1536 he achieved the high honour of being created a Knight of the Garter.

From there things went downhill, Cromwell having used his allies to get rid of Anne, later turned on them. They were accused of working to restore Princess Mary to the succession, which may have been true. Even suspected sympathies in that direction were enough to earn Cromwell's enmity, as such an eventuality would mean his death.

Cromwell persuaded Henry that Carew had been involved in a conspiracy to depose him and place Cardinal Reginald Pole on the throne, and of sympathising with Henry Courtney, Marquis of Exeter. The evidence against him consisted of treasonous letters, genuine or not, and he was tried and found guilty on 14th February 1539. He was beheaded on Tower Hill on 3rd March 1539.

Although a youthful companion and faithful servant of the King this had not saved Carew, and he fell victim to the cut-throat politics of the court. He had raised doubts about the judicial murder of Henry Courtney, and his own execution followed. Carew had married Elizabeth Bryan, and his brother-in-law Sir Francis Bryan sat on the jury that pronounced him guilty.

Chapter 13
Thomas Cromwell's
and Others

*T*homas Cromwell, *'The Hammer of the Monks'*, is one of the most unattractive and yet remarkable characters in English history. He rose to even greater heights of power and than his patron Cardinal Wolsey, and he did it without the benefit of Wolsey's precocious intellect and education. His portrait by Hans Holbein shows a soberly dressed, heavy set man with small eyes staring out in a suspicious and watchful glare. He looks like what he is: a highly intelligent man of great cunning, a fixer and a thug; not a man to be trifled with by those below him, and one who can manipulate those above him, but not one to be trusted by either group. He was the kind of man, unencumbered by principle or conscience, who thrives in any dictatorship or totalitarian regime.

Cromwell was born about 1485 in Putney the son of a sometime blacksmith,

Thomas Cromwell as shown in a Victorian engraving based on the portrait by Hans Holbein.

brewer and innkeeper. We know little about his early life but he must have received some education. He travelled in Europe from about 1504 to 1512 where he seems to have been employed as a mercenary soldier; later he appeared in Florence where he was befriended by the banker Francesco Frescobaldi. He was employed as a clerk in Antwerp, and worked for a Venetian merchant.

He visited Rome, and did business on his own account in Germany. He seems to have highly impressed his patrons, and was one of nature's businessmen, enjoying a very varied and successful career for a young man of the time.

By 1513 he was back in England where he married. Using his business acumen he became wealthy as a wool dealer and lawyer. His ability impressed Cardinal Wolsey, who employed him in 1514; and it was probably through Wolsey's influence that he served as a Member of Parliament in 1523. His skills were first used by Wolsey to suppress certain of the smaller monasteries in order for Wolsey to use their wealth to endow the colleges that he created at Ipswich and Oxford. This proved a good training ground for his later wholesale dissolution of the monasteries for Henry. He so satisfied Wolsey that he became his general factotum and secretary. If dirty work needed to be done, Cromwell could be relied on to do it.

Wolsey's failure to secure Henry VIII's divorce and his fall from favour presented Cromwell with a challenge. Initially he outwardly defended Wolsey in Parliament, but not without simultaneously building bridges with Wolsey's enemies, most notably the Duke of Norfolk, who later came to regret it. Henry was impressed with his considerable abilities, and his reputation as a man who could get things done. With Wolsey gone Cromwell stepped smoothly into the space left vacant.

Like Wolsey, Cromwell had not only ability but an enormous capacity for hard work; thereby removing that irksome and unwelcome burden from Henry; like Wolsey he would carry out Henry's orders, and offer solutions to problems, and all without objection or compunction, or being troubled by any moral niceties that others might find an impediment.

The great challenge facing him was to succeed where Wolsey failed. How to engineer Henry's divorce and his marriage to Anne Boleyn? Cromwell allied himself with Cranmer, and advised the frustrated Henry to cut the ties with Rome completely and declare himself head of the English Church by means of the Act of Supremacy. To encourage

Henry to take this drastic step Cromwell held out the double inducement of offering him unchallenged sovereignty in England, and unprecedented wealth by means of dissolving all the monasteries, and confiscating their assets.

Cromwell presided over the dissolution of the monasteries with ruthless efficiency. The monastic system was corrupt in many ways, and represented allegiance to a foreign power, the Pope in Rome; but it was also all that passed for a social support system, looking after the poor, sick and dying, and it provided a living to many common people who lived and worked on its lands. All that was swept away, along with those who dared to oppose it.

The victims included both high and low. Cromwell ensured that perjured evidence, fixed juries, guilty verdicts, and terrible executions, crushed all opposition. The centuries-old monasteries were destroyed; their lands and property confiscated and sold off at bargain prices to a new emergent class of nouveau riche administrators who owed their wealth and position to Henry - unlike the old and often discontented nobility.

Not outwardly ostentatious like Wolsey, nevertheless Cromwell accrued power and wealth, and was undoubtedly deeply corrupt, although financial corruption could be expected of anyone in an position of power in Tudor England. Henry rewarded him in a fashion unprecedented towards a commoner. He was made Privy Councillor in 1531; Chancellor of the Exchequer in 1533; Secretary of State and Master of the Rolls in 1534; and Vicar General in 1535, which ranked him above the Archbishop of Canterbury in the House of Lords. In 1536 he was created Baron Cromwell of Oakham, Knight of the Garter; Dean of Wells in 1539; and Lord Great Chamberlain in 1539. His last and greatest honour was bestowed on 17th April 1540 when he was created Earl of Essex, and elevated to the second highest level of the Peerage.

But he was headed for a fall, and it was his arrangement of Henry's disastrous marriage to Anne of Cleves in 1539 that brought him down. Having failed to bring about an alliance with France by means of a royal marriage to bolster England against the Holy Roman Emperor,

Cromwell had hoped to bring about an alliance with a German state instead. He therefore engineered the marriage with Anne of Cleves but he did not reckon with Henry's need for an attractive wife. When Henry finally met Anne in person he was, to put no finer point on it, disgusted. He reputedly described her as a *"great Flanders mare"*, and his romantic needs were more pertinent to the situation than political considerations. For Cromwell it may have been business, but for Henry it was personal.

Since Cromwell had arranged the marriage Henry looked to him to unarrange it. This should not have been to too difficult since it was never consummated and it could be annulled, not difficult to do since Henry was now Head of the Church. But Cromwell was in an intractable situation. Henry was already casting his eyes on Catherine Howard, the young niece of the Duke of Norfolk, Cromwell's enemy. Cromwell had promoted the 'new learning' of religious reform, destroyed the structures of the Catholic church, and made an enemy of the most powerful catholic in the land, the Duke of Norfolk. If he did not devise an end to the marriage he had Henry's anger to face, if he did then Henry would marry Norfolk's niece, his enemy would be in the ascendency and his days would very likely be numbered anyway.

Cromwell had miscalculated, and the sharks that circled him were ready to attack. No one liked Cromwell. He was hated as an upstart by the old nobility, by the religious conservatives, and by the common people. Just eight weeks after his elevation to his Earldom he was arrested in the Council chamber, stripped of his decorations by Norfolk and imprisoned in the Tower. He was arraigned by means of his own favourite tool, a Bill of Attainder. The Bill described him as a man of *"very base and low degree"* who had *"proved a false traitor"*. The accusations against him were of maladministration and abuse of power. But more seriously he was accused of dealing in *"weighty matters"* without the King's knowledge and presuming to have power over him. Specific accusations were made that would condemn him for Treason.

He was accused of saying, 'that some of those accused of heresy were innocent', and that 'even if the King turned from the true religious teachings he would not, and indeed he would fight for those beliefs'. He allegedly made threats against the nobility who despised him for his low birth, in that *"if the Lords handled him so he would give them such a breakfast as never was made in England and that the proudest would know"*. These allegations were most likely concoctions as they were the evidence of Sir George Throckmorton, an enemy of Cromwell's, and Sir Richard Rich who had happily perjured himself at Sir Thomas More's trial, most likely at the behest of Cromwell himself. Cromwell incriminated himself by writing to Henry from the Tower that, *"I have meddled in so many matters under your Highness that I am not able to answer them all"*. [56]

Cromwell had condemned enough people and presided over enough fixed trials to know the game was up. His grovelling pleas for mercy to Henry were made no doubt, in the hope of escaping death by hanging drawing and quartering, but also to protect his son Gregory from further retribution. Henry allowed himself to believe the accusations of heresy and treason, but mercifully allowed Cromwell to be executed by beheading on Tower Hill on 28th July 1540, albeit by a bungling axe-man. As a final insult and injury a deliberately inexperienced executioner may have been selected by Norfolk. It seems the axe struck the back of Cromwell's head rather than his neck and the executioner then spent some time hacking off his head.

However Henry soon realised the accusations against Cromwell were not all they seemed and he had been manipulated into his execution by Cromwell's enemies. He bemoaned Cromwell's fate, not out of sympathy for him but because he had lost, *"the best servant I ever had"*. Henry never found another hatchet man to match him.

Walter Hungerford, 1st Baron Hungerford of Heytsbury had the dubious distinction of accompanying Cromwell to the block, and being the first person executed under the 'Buggery Act' 1533, or to give it its proper title, The *Acte for the Punnysshement of the Vice of Buggerie*. This was the England's first civil law against sodomy, which although illegal, had previously been dealt with by the church courts. The church courts having been abolished, the situation needed to be rectified. The Act defined buggery as 'an unnatural sexual act against the will of God and man'. The offence was later defined by the courts to include only anal penetration and bestiality. This new Act was most convenient for Henry as it meant that the convicted person's wealth and possessions would be confiscated by the Crown.

Hungerford's father and grandfather had given good service to Henry VII and Henry VIII as soldiers and administrators. The young Walter was around nineteen years old at this father's death, and is recorded as having been a Squire of the Body to Henry VIII. In 1532 the father of his third wife (Elizabeth Hussey) John, Lord Hussey of Sleaford, used his influence to introduce him to Thomas Cromwell to secure for Walter the office of Sheriff of Wiltshire in 1533. Walter proved useful to Cromwell in this role and in June 1536 he was summoned to Parliament as Lord Hungerford of Heytesbury.

Hungerford's first two wives died; and his treatment of his third wife, Elizabeth, seems to have involved extreme abuse. She appealed for protection to Cromwell in 1536 complaining that her husband kept her imprisoned at Farleigh for three or four years, that he had tried to poison her, and made fruitless attempts to gain a divorce. Even in those days, when mortality rates were high, it seems bad luck for a man in his mid-thirties to already be on his third wife. Nevertheless Elizabeth's appeal to Cromwell seems to have gone unheard and he continued to protect Hungerford, who remained his protégé.

Unfortunately for them both, Cromwell fell from favour in 1540. Walter was accused of sympathising with the Pilgrimage of Grace, indeed his father-in-law, Lord John Hussey had been beheaded in 1537 for his involvement with the rebellion. Walter was also accused of employing one William Bird as Chaplain in his house while knowing him to be a traitor; and even more sinisterly, ordering another Chaplain, Hugh Wood, and one Dr Maudlin, to practice the black arts of conjuring to determine the time of the King's death (treason in itself), and his chances of defeating the northern rebels.

For good measure he was also charged with sodomy with a member of his household, and raping his daughter. Having been found guilty he was sentenced to be beheaded alongside Thomas Cromwell on 28th July 1540. Cromwell's enemies, chiefly the Duke of Norfolk, may have arranged this as an added humiliation to Cromwell who they despised. They thoughtfully arranged for Hungerford to accompany his master to the block.

Hungerford seems to have been verging on madness at his execution and while Cromwell attempted to make a dignified last speech, Walter was calling on the execution to get on with things and get it over with. If he was not mentally disturbed before he certainly seems to have been so by the time of his execution. It was reported that he *"seemed so unquiet that many judged him rather in a frenzy than otherwise"*. Who can blame him?

Giles Heron (1504-1540) was married to Sir Thomas More's youngest daughter, Cecily (born 1507). Heron's father, Sir John Heron of Hackney, had served both Henry VII and Henry VIII as Treasurer of the Chamber. When he died, Giles was still a minor and his wardship was granted to Sir Thomas More and he grew up in More's household. When he reached maturity he married Cecily More, their main residence being in Hackney, then a green and leafy place in Middlesex now a borough of London.

Giles seems to have been a somewhat rash individual. He was described as *"Wise in words, but foolish in deeds"*. For example, he refused a settlement in a court case hoping for a more favourable decision when the case was referred to his father-in-law, Sir Thomas More. This he did not get, as related in the chapter on Thomas More; happily, More's unwelcome decision does not seem to have damaged their relationship.

As Chancellor of the Duchy of Lancaster, More secured the election of his sons-in-law, Heron and Dauncey as MPs for Thetford in Norfolk in 1529, no doubt with the support of Thomas Howard 3rd Duke of Norfolk, then his ally. We know nothing of Heron's time as an MP but significantly

Thomas Cromwell did not include him on a list of those thought as being opposed to the Bill of Restraint in 1533.

Rather than coming under suspicion, Heron seems to have continued to enjoy the King's favour, as he was an Esquire of the Body, and he was probably returned to Parliament in 1536 in accordance with King's request for the re-election of the previous Members.

Heron does not enter the public record again until 1539. He had been in dispute over land with a number of his tenants, as well as with some of his relatives. It was a dispute with one of his tenants, a Master Lyons, who Heron had evicted from his farm, that led to his downfall. Lyons appears to have sought revenge by making accusations against Heron of a treasonable nature to Cromwell in February 1539. Initially things do not seem to have been too serious, and he was required to make three payments of 500 marks each to the Council when called to answer accusations. Perhaps he could not pay, as we hear of him in the Fleet prison in May, and in July he was sent to the Tower suspected of treason.

There seems to have been a flimsy case against him and the only 'witness' was Lyons, his aggrieved former tenant. The lack of evidence would not have gained a conviction in a court of law, and so Cromwell introduced a Bill of Attainder against him in the House of Lords on 3rd May 1540. This passed through all its stages in only six days. Cromwell's own fall from power delayed Heron's execution, but this did not save him and he was executed by hanging at Tyburn in August 1540.

The real reason's for Heron's execution are obscure: He was condemned by Cromwell on no real evidence, for motives we do not know; nevertheless, all accusations, trials, and Acts of Attainder for treason must have been of interest to Henry VIII, if only because they might betoken the risk of wider conspiracies, and so he must also bear responsibility for Heron's death.

Chapter 14
Catherine Howard
and Others

Catherine Howard is the most assuredly a victim, even though it is possible she might have been guilty of some of the crimes she was accused of. It is only possible to feel sympathy for her. Catherine (1521-1542) was a young girl of only nineteen when she was manipulated by her uncle the Duke of Norfolk into marriage with Henry in 1540. Henry was by then forty-nine years old, grossly overweight, with stinking ulcerated legs, and a sometimes foul and fatal temper. Catherine seems to have have had a precocious sexual appetite, and perhaps because Henry was by then not love's young dream she may have sought consolation elsewhere. She may or may not have committed adultery, but she did seek emotional consolation with others, and in her position that was the utmost folly for which she paid the ultimate price.

Catherine Howard being rowed down the Thames to the Tower as a prisoner.

Catherine was the daughter of Lord Edmund Howard, the younger brother of Thomas Howard Duke of Norfolk. Edmund was a not very successful courtier who rose to the office of Controller of Calais in 1531, and died in 1539. Catherine was one of ten orphaned children, her mother had died when she was four years old. On her father's death she was sent to live with her grandmother the Dowager Duchess of Norfolk in her house in Lambeth. Due to her uncle, the Duke's, influence she was appointed as a maid of honour to Anne of Cleves; whose marriage to Henry ended in an amicable divorce after only seven months in July 1540.

Henry most likely first met Catherine when introduced to her in Bishop Gardiner's house, an ally of the Duke of Norfolk. She caught Henry's eye, and if there is no fool like an old fool then Henry lived up to the saying and fell head over heels in love. She was said to be small and pretty, and it was her youth and vivacity that no doubt allowed Henry to think himself young again - or at least young enough to believe she might return his love. The Howards advised her to hold out for marriage.

Catherine was cynically manoeuvred into a position where the King would fall for her and marry her for her family's gain. Catherine perhaps had gone largely unnoticed in her grandmother's household; but she had a past, and one that was to catch up with her. If her uncle the Duke knew about it then he was playing a very dangerous game; but that would have been uncharacteristic of the cautious Duke, and most likely he thought her as innocent and virginal as Henry did.

Henry divorced Anne of Cleves on 9th July 1540 and married Catherine on 28th July, the same day as Thomas Cromwell's execution. The King was truly happy for the first time and lavished love and gifts on his new young wife. Despite the age difference and Henry's health problems she nevertheless seems to have done her wifely duty and satisfied his sexual desires. He showed her off in state banquets, bought her costly jewels, and gave her grants of land.

Henry was genuinely generous with those he loved or liked; and he awarded her an annual budget of the then enormous sum of £4,600. He was invigorated; and we hear that he rose early between 5am and 6am, would hear mass at 7am, and then ride until dinner time, which in those days was around 10am. But Catherine was poorly educated and could not share Henry's intellectual interests, she relied on her youthful feminine charms to keep his interest, and they had a successful marriage, or so it seemed, while it lasted.

But in February 1541 Henry fell ill again with fever perhaps due to his ulcerous legs. His pain caused him to be quick-tempered and depressed. He retreated from his usual busy social life as he sought to recuperate, and life at Hampton Court became that of an invalid and boring for the young Queen. Henry promised Catherine a grand tour of the north of his Kingdom and they embarked on it in later that year.

The royal couple progressed with an enormous retinue through the Midlands and into the North of England. This was no summer holiday but a political statement of power after the rebellions of 1537. The party reached York on 16th September, 78 days after leaving London. Catherine had not yet been crowned Queen and it was assumed she would have her coronation on the production of a child, but she remained without child, to Henry's disappointment. But nonetheless the happy couple returned to Hampton Court on 30th October.

The following day was All Saints' Day, and the King gave thanks to God, *"after sundry troubles of mind which had happened to him by marriages"*; and he prayed, *"for the good life he led and trusted to lead with his jewel of a wife"*. [57]

But Henry gave thanks too soon. At mass the following day Thomas Cranmer, the Archbishop of Canterbury, handed him a note which he begged him to read in private. Cranmer had been too frightened to tell him to his face what it contained: for it was a litany of the Queen's alleged adulterous liaisons. On reading it Henry at first refused to believe them. He ordered a discreet enquiry; but when the accusations were substantiated he became almost demented. He called for a sword so that he might kill her himself.

Catherine was accused of adultery with three gentlemen: Francis Dereham, her private secretary, Thomas Culpepper, one of the King's body servants, and Henry Mannox her music teacher. Mannox and Dereham had been with her in her grandmother's household, and she had brought Dereham with her when she became Queen. The accused were interrogated and probably tortured but they refused to admit that they had sex with Catherine after she became Queen.

Henry Mannox was her first 'lover' when she was about fourteen years old. There is no firm evidence that he accompanied after she became Queen. He was interrogated, and as far as can be ascertained only admitted to touching and feeling Katherine. A year or so later she fell in love with Francis Dereham, a gentleman of her grandmother's household. She would have married him had he not been of an inferior rank and it would not have been permitted; nevertheless they reportedly enjoyed sexual relations and referred to each other as husband and wife. Catherine did not become pregnant as a result and seems to have been quite astute in such matters since she is reported to have said she knew how a, *"a woman might meddle with a man and yet conceive no child unless she would herself"*. [58] But this could mean a variety of things.

Thomas Culpepper was known to Catherine as a distant cousin she had met in her grandmother's house. Culpepper seems to have pursued Catherine and seeing that Henry was in bad health he looked forward to a time when they would be free to marry. Catherine maintained that he had pursued her but a letter of hers to him tells a different story. She wrote in her own hand, *"when I think again that you shall depart from me again it makes my heart die to think what fortune I have that I cannot be always in your company...and thus I take my leave of you, trusting to see you shortly again and I would you were with me now that you might see the pain I take in writing to you. Yours as long as life endures, Katheryn"*. [59]

Catherine's past liaisons with Mannox and Dereham came to light when Mary Hall, a lady who had shared a bedroom with Catherine in her grandmother's house, told her brother, John Lascelles about Catherine's past activities. Lascelles had told Cranmer, who told the King. Mannox and Dereham confessed their previous sexual relations with Catherine but strenuously denied any such thing after her marriage. Culpepper and Catherine equally denied any adulterous sexual relationship, although others said that Culpepper had boasted that were the King dead, *"I am sure I might marry her"*. [60] To envisage the death of a monarch was treason.

The evidence presented something of a problem. If Catherine and Dereham had plighted their troth and called each other husband and wife when they first knew each other then a 'pre-contract' had existed; they were married in the eyes of the church, and Catherine's marriage to Henry was therefore invalid. The accused only admitted sexual relations prior to Catherine's marriage; and in the case of Culpepper not at all; only Lady Rochford's circumstantial evidence said otherwise. Culpepper refused to confess even after being tortured on the rack, but he did admit that he, *"intended and meant to do ill with the Queen, and that in likewise the Queen so would do with him"*. [61] Intent to commit adultery was not a crime as such, and in any case English Common Law discounted confessions made under torture, but in this context it was treason and this statement of intent sealed their fate if ever it was in doubt.

Catherine said that the accusations of adultery came from the wicked imagination of Lady Jane Rochford, the widow of George Boleyn executed for incestuous adultery with his sister Anne Boleyn. Lady Rochford had been Catherine's confidante and go-between and gave circumstantial evidence of adultery with Culpepper saying that he had visited Catherine's room secretly. Lady Rochford had been equally happy to supply hearsay evidence in the trial of her husband, which helped secure his execution. To overcome the evidential and legal difficulties the case was tried in Parliament and Catherine was condemned to death by an Act of Attainder.

On 10th December 1541 Culpepper was beheaded at Tyburn, and Dereham was hung drawn and quartered. The fate of Mannox is unknown. He seems to have disappeared from view after his initial interrogation. Perhaps there was nothing to charge him with? But one might think the catch-all charge of 'concealing treason' would have sufficed. Henry was never one to let a suspect go just because they were innocent. Perhaps he died under torture? Since we cannot ascertain his fate we have to give Henry the benefit of the doubt and leave him off the roll-call of the executed. Catherine was taken to the Tower of London by boat in February 1542; initially she resisted and had to be dragged on board. As they passed by London Bridge she would have seen the heads of Culpepper and Dereham displayed in the customary manner.

On 12th February 1542 Catherine was informed that she would be executed the following day. She asked for the executioner's block to be brought to her room so that she could practice kneeling at it for the executioner's blow; reconciled to her death, she wanted to go with dignity. She practised until she was satisfied. Next morning at 7am she needed some assistance to mount the scaffold on Tower Green. She made a short speech and was beheaded. She was buried along with Anne Boleyn in St Peter ad Vincula.

A number of her family members had been arrested on suspicion. She had been concerned for their safety and had written to Henry begging him to spare them. Meanwhile the Duke of Norfolk has also written to Henry fearing that, 'the abominable deeds of his nieces and the reputed treasons of many of his family members' might cause Henry to *"conceive a displeasure against him"*, [62] he disowned Catherine as he had done Anne Boleyn, and participated in both their trials. Henry did spare her family, who were either released or pardoned later. All except one that is, Lady Jane Rochford was executed for treason. Given her record as a witness against her own husband and Catherine some might think that justice of a kind.

Chapter 15
Killed With Kindness:
Arthur Plantagenet, Viscount Lisle 1542

Arthur Plantagenet was, strictly speaking, not a victim of the King and so he is not included in the roll-call of the dead in Appendix I; but his story is worth telling, and his death was caused, indirectly at least, by Henry. Arthur was an illegitmate son of Kind Edward IV (1461-1483), Henry VIII's maternal grandfather. His mother was most probably Elizabeth Lucy (née Wayte), with whom King Edward conducted one of his numerous extra-marital relationships; he was born sometime between 1461 and 1464, and was known as Arthur Wayte in his youth. [63]

Little is known of Arthur's early life but he emerges from obscurity in 1501 when he became a member of the Royal Household of his half-sister Elizabeth of York, wife of Henry VII; and on her death in 1503, Arthur became a member of the King's household. When Henry VIII became King in 1509, Arthur was appointed as an Esquire of the Body and was a trusted companion of the young King.

In 1509 Arthur was over forty-five years of age, and seems to have been mild-mannered, unassuming, easy-going character, not much suited to the shark-infested waters of Tudor politics, and an unlikely companion for the fun-loving eighteen-year-old King; perhaps Henry saw him as friendly uncle-figure and a link with his deceased mother. In any case, for the next thirty years Henry treated him well, rewarded him, and did not seem troubled or threatened by his Plantagenet name and lineage. Henry described Arthur as, *"the gentlest heart living"*. [64]

Arthur married twice. For the first time in 1511 to the Lady Elizabeth, the widow of Edmund Lord Dudley,

Henry VII's Commissioner executed by Henry VIII in 1510. Henry is believed to have arranged the marriage; no doubt thoughtfully organising a replacement spouse for Lady Elizabeth. It was through this marriage that Arthur acquired the title Viscount Lisle in 1523 and was elevated to the Peerage, with all the benefits of a landed estate. Elizabeth died in 1525/1526; and in 1529 Arthur married his second wife, another widow, Honor Grenville. Honor was around thirty years younger than Arthur, but despite the age difference their voluminous surviving correspondence shows it to have been a very happy marriage.

During these years the honours bestowed on Arthur by the King continued to flow. In 1524 he was installed as a Knight of the Garter; in 1525 appointed a Vice-Admiral of England (it was not necessary for him to know anything about ships, sailing or sea-warfare); and he was also appointed a member of the Privy Council. Not bad for an ageing uncle who might otherwise have been content to live a quiet life and avoid the fate of some of the other Plantagenets.

The coat of arms of Arthur Plantagenet, Viscount Lisle. The diagonal stripe from top right to bottom left indicates he was illegitimate.

In 1533 Arthur received his most important responsibility so far when he was appointed Governor of Calais. The port of Calais was the last remaining territory in France belonging to the English Crown. In 1534 when Henry VIII finally broke with the Papacy and established the Church of England with himself as head, the Pope was eager to bring England back into the fold by any means, including encouraging the French King Francis I to make war on the English King. The French would have liked nothing better than to retake Calais; and for any of Henry's servants to be suspected of having papist sympathies was treason.

Arthur was now carried out of his depth by currents beyond his control. The King had broken with Rome but still considered himself a catholic. His court contained two warring religious factions: the catholic conservatives led by the Duke of Norfolk, and 'new learning'-style reformers led by Thomas Cromwell. Arthur found himself caught in the middle, and tragedy ensued.

One his three chaplains, Gregory Botolf, was, unbeknown to Arthur, indeed a papist; meanwhile he made the mistake of licensing a preacher, Adam Damplip, who was an enthusiastic reformer. Arthur relied on Cromwell in London for guidance, and his own Council in Calais was becoming divided on religious doctrine. It became increasing difficult to keep order and in 1540 Henry decided decisive action was needed and Arthur was recalled to London. Henry appointed the Earl of Sussex to head a Commission to sort out the situation.

Arthur had been promoted beyond his level of competence, and initially at least it seemed that he faced just a somewhat ignominious, and probably overdue, retirement. But worse was to come. His Chaplain, Gregory Botolf was given permission to leave Calais to join Arthur in London; however he crossed the border into France. Botolf made his way to Rome where he secured money from the Pope to fund an uprising in Calais that would allow the French to make a surprise assault; but one of his co-conspirators, Clement Philpot, took fright and betrayed the plot to Earl of Sussex's Commission. Philpot was also an employee of Arthur's.

Arthur was personally interrogated by the King on his knowledge of what became known as the Botolf Plot. The King obviously not being satisfied with his answers had him securely imprisoned in the Tower of London on 19th May 1540. The conspirators were executed. The fall of Thomas Cromwell followed on 10th June, and saw his execution soon afterwards. Arthur remained languishing in prison, seemingly forgotten, for two more years. Although Henry had remarked that Arthur had gotten into trouble, *"more through simplicity and ignorance than through malice"*. [65]

In February 1542 Henry was being rowed on Thames past the Tower of London in the Royal barge when Arthur caught sight of him from the Tower battlements where he had been allowed to walk. The French Ambassador, Monsieur Marillac reported that Arthur "raised his hands high and shouted hoarsely from the Tower where he was imprisoned for mercy and release from prison. The King took it graciously and sent his secretary to the Tower to the lord to show him the King had given him his pardon, and that he would have his freedom and release from prison two or three days later, and that he would get back his possessions and offices." [66]

Arthur must have caught the King in a good mood, which was lucky considering that he had just lost his fifth wife –by cutting off her head for adultery. Perhaps seeing his aged uncle, who must now have been nearly eighty, softened his heart.

Unfortunately Arthur's luck ran out. When the King's servant, Sir Thomas Wriothesley, Cromwell's replacement, came to procure his release, Arthur was so overcome with emotion that he had a heart attack and died two days later, still in the Tower. This is the only recorded occasion when Henry managed to kill someone with kindness. Arthur's wife Honor was released from prison shortly afterwards and died a natural death in 1566.

Chapter 16
Henry Howard, Earl of Surrey

Henry Howard (1516/18-1547), the son of the Duke of Norfolk, had been treated almost like a son by Henry VIII, who had selected him as a companion for his illegitimate son Henry Fitzroy. While Henry VIII was without a legitimate male heir there was always the possibility that he would one day legitimise Fitzroy by Act of Parliament and name him as his heir apparent; being the youthful and favoured companion to a possible future king was an advantageous and potentially powerful position to be in.

Surrey was a little older than Fitzroy and was seen as something of a mentor to the young Duke. He had accompanied Fiztroy in the King's party when the King had travelled to France in 1532 to meet with Francis I. Henry was at that time cultivating good relations with the French King, and on his departure Fitzroy and Surrey remained behind as part of a diplomatic initiative to cement good relations. They spent the winter in Paris with the Francis I's three sons of similar ages, enjoying the appropriate princely pastimes. They made a good impression and were well liked. But Henry's pursuit of his divorce soured relations with the Catholic French King and the boys returned home in 1533. Fitzroy died aged seventeen in 1536.

Surrey grew to be a remarkable figure, an intelligent, educated and cultured man who still enjoys a reputation as an accomplished and original poet. He was also a man of action who served with his father the Duke of Norfolk in his military expeditions to Scotland in 1542 and in France in 1544, and in 1545 he had been appointed Governor of the captured city of Boulogne. Surrey was seemingly destined for high office but he was the grandson of the Edward Stafford, Duke of Buckingham, executed for treason in 1521 and he inherited the aristocratic pride of his ancestor. This sense of aristocratic entitlement, coupled with his rash and tempestuous nature, were dangerous characteristics for those close to the King in the final years of his reign.

A Victorian engraving of Henry Howard based on the portrait by Hans Holbein.

Some of Henry VIII's most influential councillors were low born men, some elevated by the late Thomas Cromwell's patronage. Surrey was scathing about their influence and on Cromwell's death he had declared, *"Now the false churl is dead, so ambitious of other's blood. Now he is stricken, and with his own staff"*. On being reprimanded of speaking ill of the dead he widened his attack, saying, *"These new erected men would by their wills leave no noblemen on life"*. [67] This contempt for the 'newly erected' men was shared by the Duke of Norfolk, but he was more discreet. The new men had no reason to look favourably on the arrogant Surrey who might possibly assume a position of power in the years that would follow Henry's death when his young heir Edward would reign as a minor under the protection of others.

Thus in the febrile atmosphere of the court in the closing months of Henry's reign, plot and counter-plot fermented as those closest to him positioned themselves for what might follow. Surrey fell into a trap of his own making. The late Henry Fitzroy had been married in 1533 to Surrey's sister, Mary Howard, when they were both fourteen. The Duke of Norfolk conceived of the idea of an alliance between his family and the Seymour uncles of Prince Edward so that both families could dominate the government. Mary would marry Sir Thomas Seymour, brother of the late Queen Jane, an idea she does not seem to have been keen on.

In December 1546, one of the Kings 'new men' Sir Richard Southwell informed the Privy Council that he, *"knew certain things of the Earl that touched his fidelity to the King"*. [68] In response Surrey offered to fight Southwell in a duel, but instead he was arrested and placed in the Tower. Likewise his father the Duke was called to London and placed in custody. The following investigation uncovered the proposed pact between the Howards and Seymours - and worse.

Surrey had a more audacious plan which was to instruct his sister that when she was inevitably interviewed by the King about the proposed marriage to Seymour she should seduce him and become his mistress. Mary was even less impressed by that idea. But Surrey likened the outcome of such a relationship to the power that the French King's mistress, Madame d'Etampes had over him. Henry VIII was not surprisingly outraged by the idea. He personally made notes on the case, which included, *"If a man compassing himself to govern the realm do actually go about to rule the King and should for that purpose advise his daughter or his sister to become his harlot... What this importeth?"* To Henry it importeth treason!

Henry VIII, himself on the edge of death drew up the charge sheet in his own, now unsteady, hand. Perhaps to spare himself embarrassment, he decided to indict Surrey on more technical charges of treason. These were that he had incorporated into his own coat of arms those of Edward the Confessor (King of England 1042-1066); that he had replaced the coronet in his arms with a crown; and that he had displayed the arms of his supposed royal ancestors in the glass in the windows of this house. As a collateral descendent of the Plantagenets, Surrey was entitled to bear the arms of England in the second quarter of his shield, but he had displayed them in the first quarter, which was the sole right of the heir apparent to the throne. [69]

This might seem like a bit of heraldic vanity to the modern mind but in those days it was a clear signal of the assertion of his royal pretensions. The Duke of Norfolk's mistress, Bess Holland, gave evidence that Surrey had said of the King that he was, *"much grown in his body and could not go up and down stairs...that his Majesty was sickly and could not long endure"*. [70] While this was quite true, it was treason to speak of the King's death, and as Henry faced what he must have known was his impending end he had no intention of leaving any threats, real or imagined, to impede his heir's succession.

Surrey was tried on 13th January 1547 and put up a spirited defence. When the inevitable sentence was handed down Surry allowed himself one last outburst, *"I know that the King wants to get rid of the noble blood round him and employ none but low people"*. There was a strong element of truth in that, and those low men intended to protect their positions. The verdict was a forgone conclusion and he was sentenced to death. He was helped on his way to the block by his own father, the Duke of Norfolk who on the 12th January had made a formal confession admitting that he had concealed his son's treason. A Bill of Attainder was passed against father and son. Henry died on 27th January 1547 before he was able to sign the Duke's death warrant.

Surrey had indeed been the victim of a conspiracy by the 'low men' among Henry's government, but he had been hoist on the petard of his own rashness. His closeness to the King's late son Fitzroy and Henry's own affection for him in his youth had not been enough to save him when the survival of the royal dynasty was in question. Surrey was beheaded on 19th January 1547, just nine days before the King's own death.

Chapter 17
The Ones That Got Away – Almost

Cardinal Wolsey

Thomas Wolsey was a remarkable man by anyone's standards. He rose from the humblest beginnings to become the second most powerful and richest man in the kingdom. He was the son of Robert Wolsey of Ipswich; the year of his birth is uncertain and is variously given as between 1471 or 1473. Wolsey is often cited as being the son of a butcher, but this story arose in court gossip; his contemporary biographer George Cavendish calls him only an *"honest poor man's son"*. [71] Certainly Robert was wealthy enough to provide young Thomas with a good education. He had a precocious intellect and aged only eleven was sent to Magdalen College Oxford where at the age of fifteen he took his diploma of Bachelor of Arts, earning himself the soubriquet of the Boy Bachelor.

Wolsey took holy orders and remained at the college as the Master of the school attached to the college until 1500. As Bursar he displayed his passion for show and magnificence by spending a large amount of college funds on completing Magadalen Tower, an extravagance resented by his fellows. He was forced to resign his post but found a good position with the Marquis of Dorset whose sons had been his pupils. Residing now in Limington, Somerset, he displayed another facet of his character when having drunk too much at a fair he was confined to the stocks for disorderly conduct by the local landowner Sir Amyas Paulet. He never forgot the slight to his dignity and exacted a (non fatal) revenge of Sir Amyas many years later.

In 1501 Wolsey became chaplain to Henry Dean, Archbishop of Canterbury, and in 1506 a royal chaplain acting as secretary to Richard Fox (1448-1528) Bishop of Winchester. Wolsey was now in a position to impress King Henry VII with his abilities, which he duly did. In 1508 He undertook a diplomatic mission to Scotland, and later that year another one to the Flanders to discuss a possible marriage between the widowed King, and Margaret, daughter of the Emperor Maximilian. Henry VII was sufficiently pleased with Wolsey's competence and efficiency to award him the deanery of Lincoln, which was the beginning of his amassing a vast fortune.

The accession of Henry VIII in 1509 gave Wolsey an unprecedented opportunity which he fully exploited. With the aid of his patron Bishop Fox, he was in 1511 appointed the King's Almoner and a member of the King's Council. Wolsey made himself indispensable to Henry, and very quickly got the measure of the twenty year old monarch, who Cavendish tells us was, *"young and lusty, disposed all to mirth and pleasure and to follow his desire and appetite, not caring to toil in the busy affairs of the realm".*[72] Wolsey was only too pleased to toil in the busy affairs of the realm, a job totally suited to his intellect, abilities, ambition and inclination. Not only that but as Cavendish goes on to tell, the King esteemed him because he would, "advance the King's mere will and pleasure, without any respect to the case in question". [73] As the most capable man in the council Wolsey quickly rose to pre-eminence.

Wolsey organised the King's expedition for war with France in 1513 and was rewarded with the Bishopric of the captured town of Tournai. In the following year he was made Bishop of Lincoln and of York. His attentions now turned to international relations and he pursued a policy designed to make England a prime player in continental politics, a policy he pursued until his downfall. Continental politics from 1519, and for the next quarter of a century, were about the rivalry between Francis I of France and the Holy Roman Emperor Charles V. Wolsey tried, unsuccessfully, to make England hold the balance of power between the two.

In 1518 the Treaty of London was almost the greatest diplomatic triumph of Wolsey's career. The treaty was a non-aggression pact and defensive alliance between all the major European powers: England, France, the Holy Roman Empire, the Holy See, Spain, Burgundy and the Netherlands: a sort of proto NATO, intended to unite Christendom against the Islamic (Turkish) threat. Unfortunately after only three years the idea collapsed when Spain and the Holy Roman Empire had attacked France, and Henry VIII joined the war in an attempt to re-conquer England's historic lands in France.

Nevertheless honours, appointments and their revenues continued to fall upon Wolsey thick and fast: he was appointed Bishop of Bath and Wells 1518, Durham 1523, Winchester 1529, as well as being given a multitude of other sources of income. Wolsey was avaricious and made himself the second richest man in the kingdom after the King. Tudor politics were corrupt and anyone seeking office expected to bribe those from whom they sought favours (with the notable exception of Sir Thomas More), and to be bribed upon attaining office.

Wolsey loved architecture and to display his wealth; he therefore built the most magnificent palace in the land, Hampton Court. Cavendish tells us that he was served by a small army of 500 retainers and servants.

In 1515 Wolsey had been made Lord Chancellor, the highest governmental office in the land; and to satisfy Henry's demands at home and abroad Wolsey had the task of raising the necessary funds. He made such large demands in taxation that he became hated by the common people and the nobility in equal measure. In 1524-1529 as a money raising measure he dissolved about thirty monasteries with fewer than seven inmates and took their assets. This was done with the approval of Rome, and paved the way for the full dissolution under Cromwell a few years later.

In 1515 Henry had used his influence to secure Wolsey the office of Cardinal, and in 1517 he again used that influence to make an unwilling Pope Leo X appoint Wolsey as Cardinal-Legate in England. Wolsey now operated as the Pope's representative in England, and indeed he had eyes on the papacy itself. Still in the King's favour Wolsey attempted, with Henry's support, to win the papacy when it fell vacant in 1521, and again in 1523, each time with false promises of support from Charles V. This must have been the summit of his career: a poor commoner from Ipswich was second only to the King; Dukes and nobles had to do his bidding and feared his displeasure; and he was within reach of the papacy. Had he been successful he would have been only the second Englishman in history to achieve it. But things were about to go badly wrong.

Wolsey had few if any real friends and was dependent entirely on the King's favour for his survival. By 1527 the King needed a divorce from Katherine of Aragon and Wolsey had the task of delivering it. Wolsey may himself have raised the question of the validity of the King's marriage, well aware that the lack of a male heir was a potentially destabilising factor and that Henry needed a way out. In ordinary times obtaining a Papal dispensation to annul the marriage would have been

well within his diplomatic capabilities. But Pope Clement VII lived in mortal fear of Katherine of Aragon's nephew Charles V and was simply not in a position to grant one. By 1529 when it was obvious that Henry would have to take matters into his own hands, Wolsey fell from favour.

Henry dismisses Wolsey from all his government positions, though Wolsey was allowed to remain Archbishop of York.

Wolsey's enemies among the nobility turned upon him. He was denied access to the King. The Dukes of Norfolk and Suffolk poisoned the King's mind against him further. He was dismissed as Lord Chancellor and packed off to his bishopric of York. He had never formally been installed as Bishop and set about organising his enthronement as though he could somehow hang on to the good times. This was seen as a formal challenge to the King. Wolsey was accused of treason, and an indictment was raised against him by the King's attorney in the Court of King's Bench for receiving bulls from Rome in contravention of the Statutes of Praemunire (see Glossary). Wolsey also made representations to the French King and Holy Roman Emperor to help save his skin, and these were looked upon as treasonable.

Sir William Kingston was dispatched to bring Wolsey back to the Tower of London to face a treason trial. The story goes that many years before a fortune-teller and told Wolsey that he would meet his end by Kingston. Wolsey took it to mean the place, Kingston-upon-Thames, and in travelling from his palace in Hampton Court had studiously avoided ever setting his foot in the nearby town. When Sir William appeared in York with an armed retinue to take him to London Wolsey felt the prophesy was coming true. The party made their way as far as Leicester Abbey where Wolsey now old, tired and ill took to his death-bed. Cavendish records his last lament before dying on 29th November 1530, *"If I had served God as diligently as I have done the King, He would not have given me over in my grey hairs"*.

Had Wolsey made his way to the Tower then there can be little doubt that he would have been tried for treason, convicted and beheaded. Henry had no sentimental attachments even to his oldest and most loyal servants if they could not support him in the momentous changes he needed to make, or posed even a potential threat. Wolsey was unloved and unlamented, with the exception perhaps of Thomas Cromwell who knew his true worth, and to whom he owed his own advancement. But Wolsey's high handed ways and avarice paved the way for the wave of anti-clericalism that allowed Henry to sweep away a thousand years of church tradition. Nevertheless, Wolsey's abilities and accomplishments were truly remarkable.

Cardinal Reginald Pole

Reginald Pole was the son of Margaret Countess of Salisbury and Sir Richard Pole. Margaret was the daughter of George Duke of Clarence, Shakespeare's, *"false, fleeting, perjured Clarence"*, and Isabel Neville, daughter of the Richard Neville Earl of Warwick, the 'Kingmaker' who helped set Edward IV on the throne. Clarence had been executed in the Tower of London in 1478 on the orders of his brother Edward IV. Edward was not a cruel or vindictive man but of necessity he had on occasion to be ruthless. According to tradition, and Shakespeare, George Duke of Clarence chose to die in the Tower by being drowned in a butt of malmsey wine.

Reginald was born in March 1500 in Staffordshire. His royal blood gave him a claim to the English throne that was arguable stronger than that of the Tudors. His lineage certainly made him a person of great interest to the Crown. He was initially educated by Carthusian monks at West Sheen just outside London, and at the age of twelve he enrolled at Magdalene College, Oxford. At the age of nineteen he went to Italy to continue his studies at the University of Padua funded by Henry VIII. He returned to England in 1525 and was high in Henry's favour as the King valued learning and scholarship; his mother was greatly esteemed by Queen Catherine of Aragon. All was going well until the issue of the King's divorce arose.

Reginald first appeared to favour the arguments for the annulment and in 1530 he was sent to the University of Paris to obtain a decision favourable to the King. Henry had hoped to obtain judgements from various learned bodies endorsing his request that the Pope annul his marriage on the grounds he had married his brother's wife. However Reginald became disenchanted with the radical policies pursued by Thomas Cromwell which eventually led to the break with Rome. On the death of Cardinal Wolsey in November 1530 he was offered the Archbishopric of York but refused it.

Henry did not turn against him at this point but allowed him to leave the country in 1532, and he made his way to

Rome. Here he became part of the intellectual circles that sought to pursue the reforms necessary to reconcile the Lutherans with the Church of Rome. He was a friend of the artist Michelangelo, himself a deeply religious man who may also have had reformist leanings, but if he did he wisely kept them to himself in counter-Reformation Rome. Before long the ideological and doctrinal divides promoted by Cromwell on Henry's behalf proved too much for Pole to bridge.

Matters came to a head in 1535 when Henry demanded that he declare his position to the divorce. Pole had responded by means of a violent letter to the King which he later expanded into the treatise, *Pro Ecclesiasticae Unitatis Defensione* (Defending the Unity of the Church). He attacked Henry on the two key issues closest to his heart: his divorce from Queen Katherine, and his assumption of supreme authority over the Church of England. Henry reacted equally violently; he stopped Pole's pension and income from his ecclesiastical offices. Furthermore, he arrested and interrogated Pole's relatives and imprisoned his aged mother Margaret in the Tower; leading to her eventual execution in 1541.

Pope Paul III responded by making Pole a Cardinal in December 1536. Henry then secured from Parliament a Bill of Attainder against Pole and put a price on his head. Had Henry been able to lay hands on Pole there can be little doubt that his severed head would have adorned Tower Bridge.

On the death of Pope Paul III in 1549, Pole came close to being elected Pope, losing by only two votes to Pope Julius III. If had been successful he would have been only the second Englishman to become Pope, and would have had the remarkable distinction to being the only Pope who also had a valid claim to the English throne. In 1555 he could have again been a contender but lost to Pope Marcellus II (who reigned for only three weeks in April), and then to Pope Paul IV, who became his bitter enemy; however, by then he was back in England.

To cut a long story short. After Henry had executed many martyrs who could not quite understand his still being a Catholic and yet denying the authority of the pope at the same time, he died in 1547, and was succeeded by his nine year old son Edward VI, who died just six years later at the age of 15. Edward had been a firmly Protestant king. In 1553 he was in turn succeeded by his elder sister Mary. Mary I was an old-style catholic. Pole was welcomed back to help her identify and burn the real heretics - the Protestants.

After Archbishop Cranmer was burnt at the stake in 1556, Pole succeeded him as Archbishop of Canterbury. However, just to prove that you cannot please everyone however hard you try, Pope Paul IV then accused Pole of heresy and summoned him to Rome for an appointment with the Inquisition. Pole was saved by Mary's intervention, and then had the good sense to die sixteen hours after her in 1558, before the Protestant Elizabeth I could succeed, and matters could get any worse.

Catherine Parr

Catherine Parr was Henry's sixth and last wife who managed to survive long enough to become his widow. She was born in 1512 the eldest child of Sir Thomas and Maude Greene of Kendal Castle in Westmorland. Her father died when she was just five years old. In 1529 she married at the age of seventeen to Edward Borough, most likely a much older man, who died in 1532. Catherine then married Sir John Neville, Lord Latimer who was aged about forty. They lived in Snape Castle in Yorkshire, where Sir John died in 1543 after a long illness. Neither of the marriages produced any children.

Catherine had served as a Gentlewoman of the Chamber to Catherine Howard until her fall in 1542 when she returned to Yorkshire to supervise the upbringing of her three step-children. She had been left a wealthy widow and at the young age of thirty-two would not have been short of suitors. Sir Thomas Seymour, uncle to the heir to the throne, had cast his eye on her and offered marriage. Catherine was tempted by the rakish Sir Thomas but before the offer could be accepted the King made known his interest in the lady, and the King could not be denied what he wanted.

Catherine was a highly educated and intelligent woman with an interest in religion and the new teachings of reform. She had strong connections at court; her mother Maude had been a Lady-in-Waiting to Katherine of Aragon, and she had been educated with the young Princess Mary. But she was not reported as beautiful, particularly sparkling or witty, the kind of things that usually attracted Henry; and neither was she young considering the ages of his last three wives. But she was it seems warm and kind by nature and had nursed two older husbands through long illnesses; and perhaps Henry was looking more for a companion and a nurse rather than another torrid sexual partner.

After Catherine Howard's execution in February 1542 Henry grew fatter and depressed. Norfolk's success in battle against the Scots in the winter of 1542 cheered him up enough for him to summon Princess Mary for the Christmas celebrations. The following summer of 1543, after eighteen months of bachelorhood, he surprised everyone by announcing his sixth marriage to Catherine Parr. They were married by Bishop Gardiner at Hampton Court. Catherine was devout, and her inclinations when not home-building for the King, were for religious reform rather than outright Lutheran revolution.

Catherine gathered scholars of the new teachings around her and by 1545 this gave rise to questions about her theological soundness. Henry asked Bishop Gardiner, a religious conservative to examine Catherine on her religious views. Henry may also have come to resent being lectured on religion by his wife. He reportedly said to her, *"You have become a doctor Kate, to instruct us, as we take it, and not to be instructed or directed by us"*. [74] Gardiner was only too pleased to draw up charges against the Queen and to send her to the block on behalf of the religious conservatives he represented.

A copy of Gardiner's report found its way to Catherine, probably from a well-wisher, which allowed her to make a pre-emptive strike and throw herself on Henry's mercy. She assured the King that she only wanted to raise questions on religion in order to distract Henry from his illness and pain and learn from his superior knowledge. Henry was flattered and reassured, he forgave his wife and all was well again. At that point Sir Thomas Wroithesley came with a detachment of guards to arrest her, but he found the royal couple walking arm in arm. Henry sent Wroithesley packing, driving him away with the insults of, *"arrant knave, beast and fool"*. [75]

Catherine had learnt her lesson, she nursed Henry, kept a low profile and survived. Henry died in January 1547, and Catherine was free to marry Sir Thomas Seymour, who may have been her preferred choice in 1543. After three childless marriages and at the age of thirty-five she conceived her first child. Catherine gave birth to her daughter Mary on 30th August 1548, but she sadly died of a post-natal fever on 7th September.

Thomas Howard, 3rd Duke of Norfolk

Thomas Howard (1473-1554) was the consummate great survivor of Henry's reign, and indeed of the entire Tudor period; he survived many a crisis that would have seen a lesser man lose his head, before dying of natural causes at the ripe old age of 81 in the reign of Mary I.

The Howard family had been awarded the Dukedom of Norfolk in the mid 15th century; and despite the Howards' view of themselves as natural aristocrats their pedigree can only traced back to Sir William Howard, a Chief Justice of the Common Pleas (civil law courts) in the reigns of Edward I and Edward II. Sir John Howard, the grandson of Sir William, was Admiral of the King's Navy in the North of England, and Sheriff of Norfolk. He owned a substantial amount of land in the county, which was greatly increased when his grandson, Sir Robert married an heiress of the ancient house of Mowbray, the Dukes of Norfolk. Sir

Robert's son Sir John Howard was a leading supporter of the House of York in the Wars of the Roses and was rewarded by Edward IV with the Dukedom of Norfolk, the title then being vacant.

John Howard went on to serve Richard III and died fighting at the battle of Bosworth in 1485. Henry VII attainted the Howards so that John's heir, Thomas, lost the Dukedom and spent three years imprisoned in the Tower of London. But his abilities and experience as an administrator and soldier went a long way in persuading the King of his usefulness, and Thomas obtained a reverse of the Acts of Attainder against himself and his late father. Thomas Howard, restored as the Earl of Surrey, was an able general and went on to serve Henry VIII, most notably when he led the English army to a complete victory over the Scottish invasion force at Flodden in 1513. Howard annihilated the Scottish army, including its King James IV and the flower of its aristocracy, and as a reward was made 2nd Duke of Norfolk in 1514; and died in 1524.

His son, Thomas Howard, the 3rd Duke, had a long and distinguished career under Henry VIII. He served as Lord Lieutenant in Ireland 1520-1522, and Lord High Treasurer from 1522. Howard was the man that Henry called on when there were practical things to be done of a military, and sometimes a distasteful, nature. It was Norfolk who put down the rebellions of 1537; he complained, justifiably, about the lack of men and arms available to counter the serious threat of forty thousand armed rebels, but through the King's dissembling with the rebel leaders he gained time and was able to muster the forces necessary to crush them. Henry may not have liked or trusted Norfolk but he understood him well enough to know how to use him.

Norfolk was proudly aristocratic but realistic and fiercely ambitious to hold on to that which he thought his due. He led the religious conservatives but nevertheless gained what he could materially through the suppression of the monasteries. He resented the low-born status of Wolsey but had to respect and recognise his abilities. He bided his time until Wolsey fell from grace and was then able to turn on him. He showed his vindictiveness in the long list of crimes that he drew up against Wolsey, including that had tried to infect the King with venereal disease by breathing on him. Even Henry baulked at this and revised a more believable set of charges.

Norfolk initially supported Cromwell's rise to power, but soon came to regret it when the master manipulator achieved a position so powerful when he could put anyone's safety in jeopardy. But again, Howard bided his time and turned on Cromwell when in due course his turn came to fall from favour. On Cromwell's arrest he took pleasure in ripping the chains of office from around his neck and in the blows that accompanied him as he was conveyed to the Tower.

Howard had tried to convince Sir Thomas More to sign the Act of Supremacy and save his life; and his remark to More exactly conveys his view of the subject, "It is perilous striving with princes, and therefore I would wish you somewhat to incline to the King's pleasure. By God's body Master More – the anger of the prince means death". [76] Whatever his religious conservative views may have been, Howard had no intention of letting them get in the way of his own survival.

Norfolk had been happy to push two female members of his immediate family into Henry's orbit, in the form of Anne Boleyn and Catherine Howard, in order that he and his family might benefit from their position as Queen. It had not taken long for both these marriages to go disastrously wrong, but Howard miraculously survived the disgrace, and indeed served on the juries in the House of Lords that condemned both of his nieces to death.

Norfolk had fallen out with his own wife Elizabeth, and installed his mistress, Bess Holland in his house. His disgraceful treatment of his wife was something of a national scandal, that even Henry had to reprimand him. In an age of arranged marriages this was not perhaps surprising, but his wife's remark about him, even allowing for her partial view of matter, sums up an important facet of his character, *"I will never trust my husband, he can speak fair to his enemy as to his friend"*. [77] He had the ability to face whichever way was needed to ensure his own benefit.

His services were still needed, and in 1542 not long after he was lucky to survive the debacle of Catherine Howard's marriage and execution, he was called upon to lead an expedition into Scotland. This resulted in the English victory of the battle of Solway Moss on 25th November after a short war that was the result of religious differences and Scotland's alliance with France.

The Scottish army was routed by the Duke and news of the defeat is said to have caused King James V a nervous breakdown, leading to his death. This news cheered up a disconsolate Henry VIII still brooding on Catherine Howard, and it demonstrated Norfolk's usefulness once again. Norfolk led another army for Henry in 1545, this time into France, although without such spectacular success on that occasion.

As Henry's health declined and his paranoia not unreasonably increased, Norfolk's position became more unstable. The ill-judged activities of his son Henry Howard, Earl of Surrey, let to his trial for treason. His father was prepared to admit his son's guilt in order to try and save his own neck. Surrey was condemned to death and executed. Norfolk was likewise found guilty of treason and condemned to death. Only Henry's own death before he was able to sign the death warrant saved Norfolk's life.

Norfolk remained a prisoner in the Tower during the reign of Edward VI but was released on the accession of Mary I in 1553. Although a very old man by the standards of the time he was still able to serve his monarch in the usual fashion. He presided over the trial of the Duke of Northumberland for treason and his execution on Tower Green. Norfolk commanded one last military action against Sir Thomas Wyatt's Rebellion in 1554 which ended in a humiliating failure, and he died later that year.

Hans Holbein's portrait of Norfolk of around 1539 shows a proud and craggy faced man holding his staffs of office, and looking broadly built in his Tudor costume. But this was the painter's art triumphing over nature. Norfolk was reportedly, *"small and spare of stature"*. [78] But there was nothing small about his ambitions. The Howards had worked their way back from defeat and disgrace in 1485 and the 3rd Duke had no intention of allowing his family fortunes to flounder again. He was an arrogant aristocrat but he had the wit to bend with the wind, bide his time, and do anything that was necessary to survive, including sacrificing members of his family. He survived by the skin of his teeth, and the Howards still enjoy the Dukedom of Norfolk today.

Chapter 18
Henry VIII: The Verdict

Henry VIII was without doubt, selfish, egotistical, cruel, and callous; he was also highly intelligent, educated, accomplished, charming, charismatic, and generous. He displayed enough of the characteristics necessary to indicate that he possessed a psychopathic personality. It is impossible to find evidence that he ever expressed regret or remorse for those he killed, or even empathy with their sufferings.

Much has been made about the golden promise of his youth, but the darker characteristics of his later years were clearly displayed early on in his reign. He ruthlessly executed Empson and Dudley, Edmund de la Pole, and the Duke of Buckingham, knowing full well they were innocent of any real crimes; and he allowed William de la Pole to rot in the Tower of London from the beginning to the end of his reign, merely for the 'crime' of having been born with an arguably better claim to the throne.

A family portrait painted after Henry's death shows him with his children Edward, Elizabeth (right) and Mary, together with Mary's husband Philip of Spain.

The Tudor era saw the end of the Middle-Ages and beginning of the modern era. The Wars of the Roses saw the end of the entrenched power of the feudal aristocracy; and had Henry VII or Henry VIII been weak monarchs that power might have seen a temporary revival, but whatever else they were they were not weak. Henry VII began the changes by outlawing the private armies of the aristocrats, and promoting 'new men' of lower class to high rank in government: men who depended on the King for their wealth and position, not their birth.

Henry VIII enthusiastically continued that policy; and there were complaints, justified from their point of view, from the old aristocrats. Those unwise enough to make too much of the issue, like Buckingham and Surrey, lost their heads. Most of Henry's most effective servants had been low born men such as Wolsey, More, and Cromwell. As Henry himself said in 1545, he *"would not be bound to be served by nobles, but by such men, whatsoever their status, as I would appoint to office"*. [79] That may have been something of an exaggeration since he still had to take the aristocracy into account, but the change in government was real enough.

A more radical revolution happened almost by chance. Had Katherine of Aragon presented Henry with a healthy son and heir, or better still a brood of sons, Henry would have most likely remained a conventional Catholic King, albeit an adulterous one. Had Katherine's nephew, Charles V, not held Pope Clement VII a virtual captive in Rome, the Pope would have granted Henry the divorce he craved. But circumstances conspired against him. Henry's personal problem brought to the boil an issue that had simmered for the previous three hundred years: the matter of jurisdiction and sovereignty in England between King and Pope.

It is characteristic of English Common Law that what might be in itself a small dispute can give rise to a judgement of momentous importance. The question in hand was only the legal validity of one marriage but the real issue at stake was who held power in England? Henry resolved that it was English law and him, not the Pope and the law of the Church. Once Henry set his mind on a course of action, the added allure of complete sovereignty in his own land, and the acquisition of the Church's wealth (and being free to marry his sweetheart of course), made him unstoppable.

With hindsight we might underestimate the magnitude of what Henry achieved in his break from Rome. It is remarkable that he did not face more organised opposition. He overturned a social order that had existed since Anglo Saxon times, and a power structure that had existed since 1066. Previous monarchs had just tinkered with the problem. It might be argued that only a ruler with a psychopathic personality, devoid of conscience and prepared to be as ruthless as Henry was could have achieved such a revolution in the seven brief years from 1529 to 1536. Some other European countries took the next three or four centuries to free themselves from the overt political influence of the Catholic Church.

To destroy the monastic system and set aside the authority of the Pope and the Catholic Church, Henry needed the callousness necessary to sacrifice old friends and councillors, and the cruelty to condemn anyone who resisted to horrific deaths, thereby instilling fear in those who might be tempted to rebel. Those who did rebel were mercilessly crushed. The Pilgrimage of Grace represented a very real threat to his reign. The rebels were however innately conservative and only wanted a return to the old ways under the old aristocracy, and it was that conservatism that defeated

them. It enabled Henry to lie to them, gain time, gather his strength, and then crush them. He emerged stronger than ever.

Henry preferred to leave the tedious job of day to day administration to his chief ministers while he enjoyed himself, but it was a mistake to underestimate him. He reputedly had a phenomenal memory, able to recall the names of all his royal servants, and the details of every grant of land he ever made. He scrutinised and annotated state documents with comments; he attended debates in the House of Lords (hopefully more interesting then than they are now); and gave many personal interviews to foreign ambassadors. Those he executed were a combination of the rash, the rebellious, the principled, the religiously committed, and in many cases the innocent. Cromwell was his attack dog, but Henry held the leash.

Henry was an early exponent of Stalin's doctrine of 'no man, no problem'. And like Stalin, he also allowed the excesses he required to implement his policies to be carried out by unscrupulous servants who could be sacrificed later; in his case, Wolsey and then Cromwell. Also like Stalin, certainly in his later years, he ruled his advisors by creating an atmosphere of distrust and fear, whereby they sought to preserve themselves by being ever ready to inform on and condemn their colleagues.

Despite his excesses Henry maintained his popularity with his people to the end of his reign. Even the rebels of 1537 saw him as a good king led astray by evil councillors. A delusion he was happy for them to hold, while it benefitted him. Even so, Henry never lost the love and admiration of his people because he was to them a typically English King, in appearance, manner and character. He defended England against outside domination and threat. Weak kings never fared well and Henry was a strong king. The English saw him as one of their own.

Two days before his death Henry drew up his will, and named those he wished to be on his nine year old son Edward's, Council of Regency. Henry left off the name of the vindictive and vicious Bishop Gardiner who had served him well in maintaining orthodox religious doctrine and persecuting the religious reformers and heretics. His councillor, Sir Anthony Denny, knelt by his bed and asked if the King had left off the Bishop's name by mistake?

Henry answered, *"Hold your peace. I remember him well enough, and of good purpose have left him out; for surely, if he were in my testament, and one of you, he would cumber you all and you would never rule him, he is so troublesome a nature. Marry, I myself could use him and rule him to all manner of purposes as seemed good unto me; but so shall you never do".* [80] Quite so, only Henry could have ruled the nest of vipers that was the Tudor court and he held them in his sway until the end. They may have manipulated him on occasion but he held the ultimate sanction – to cut off their heads,

Henry did the right things, perhaps for the wrong reasons; but without his characteristics of callousness, cruelty and lack of conscience or remorse, he would not have been able to force through his radical agenda. That agenda was to the great benefit of the English nation. It freed us from the influence and power of a foreign potentate. It established England as a fully independent nation state. England, a small and sparsely populated country in relation to the other great European states nonetheless embarked on its successful four hundred year foreign policy of influencing the balance of power in Europe in order to maintain her own freedom and independence.

Henry's figure has be-strode English history for five hundred years. He did his best to create a tyrannical government to serve his own ends; but ironically his revolution meant that Parliamentary government developed in a way he would not have foreseen, or no doubt have approved of. He needed Parliament to implement all his revolutionary measures; it was an instrument of his tyranny, but this nevertheless led to the assertion of its own power later.

Less than twenty years after Henry's death Sir Thomas Smith wrote in 1565, *"The most high and absolute power in the realm of England consisteth in the Parliament. The Parliament abrogateth old law, maketh new, giveth order for things past and for things thereafter to be followed, changeth rights and possessions of private men, legitmateth bastards, establish forms of religion, altereth weights and measures, giveth forms of succession to the crown. And the consent of Parliament is taken to be every man's consent".* [81]

The continuous thread that runs through English history from thirteenth century down to today is the development of Parliamentary government. Henrys' break with Rome was an important step in that development. For 439 years from 1534 to 1973 no laws could be made in England except by Parliament. The last sentence in Sir Thomas Smith's quotation gives expression to everything that Parliament was until 1st January 1973 when it surrendered its sovereignty to the European Economic Community*. Few rulers have left such a long-lasting legacy, intentional or not.

*European Economic Community / European Community / European Union / The Union

Appendix

Henry VIII's Main Victims in Chronological Order

1. **Sir Richard Empson**, beheaded 17th August 1510

2. **Edmund Dudley**, beheaded 17th August 1510

3. **Edmund de la Pole**, 6th Earl of Suffolk, beheaded April 1513

4. **Edward Stafford**, 3d Duke of Buckingham, beheaded 17th May 1521

5. **Elizabeth Barton**, plus five others, 20th April 1534

6. **John Fisher,** Bishop of Rochester, beheaded 22nd June 1535

7. **Sir Thomas More**, beheaded 17th July 1535

8. **John Houghton**, Prior of Charterhouse, hung, drawn and quartered 4th May 1535

9. **Robert Lawrence**, Prior of Beauvale Charterhouse, hung, drawn and quartered 4th May 1535

10. **Augustine Webster**, Prior of Axholme Charterhouse, hung, drawn and quartered 4th May 1535

11. **William Exmere**, Procurator of Charterhouse, London, hung, drawn and quartered 19th June 1535

12. **Humphrey Middlemore**, Vicar of Charterhouse, London, hung, drawn and quartered 19th June 1535

13. **Sebastian Newdigate**, monk, Charterhouse, London, hung, drawn and quartered 19th June 1535

14. **Richard Reynolds**, Prior of Syon Abbey, hung, drawn and quartered, 19th June 1535

15. **John Haile,** Priest, hung, drawn and quartered, 19th June 1535

16. **George Boleyn**, Lord Rochford, beheaded 17th May 1536

17. **Sir Henry Norris**, beheaded, 17th May 1536

18. **William Bereton**, beheaded 17th May 1536

19. **Mark Smeaton**, beheaded 17th May 1536

20. **Anne Boleyn** 1536, beheaded, 19th May 1536

21. **John Rochester**, monk, Charterhouse, London, hung in chains until dead, York, 11th May 1537

22. **James Walworth**, monk, Charterhouse, London, hung in chains until

dead, York 11th May 1537

23. **William Greenwood**, lay brother, Charterhouse, London, starved to death, Newgate prison, 6th June 1537

24. **John Davey**, deacon and monk, Charterhouse, London, starved to death, Newgate prison, 8th June 1537

25. **Robert Salt**, lay brother, Charterhouse, London, starved to death, Newgate prison, 9th June 1537

26. **Walter Pierson**, lay brother, Charterhouse, London, starved to death, Newgate prison, 10th June 1537

27. **Thomas Green**, alias Thomas Greenwood, monk, Charterhouse, London, starved to death, Newgate prison, 10th June 1537

28. **Thomas Scryven**, lay brother, Charterhouse, London, starved to death, Newgate prison, 15th June 1537

29. **Thomas Redyng**, lay brother, Charterhouse, London, starved to death, Newgate prison, 16th June 1537

30. **Richard Bere**, monk, Charterhouse, London, starved to death, Newgate prison, 9th August 1537

31. **Thomas Johnson**, monk, Charterhouse, London, starved to death, Newgate prison, 20th September 1537

32. **Robert Aske**, Leader of the Pilgrimage of Grace, hanged, York, 1537

33. **Thomas Darcy**, 1st Baron Darcy, Pilgrimage of Grace, beheaded, Tower Green, 1537

34. **John Lord Hussey**, Butler of England, Pilgrimage of Grace, beheaded, 1537

35. **John Hallam**, beheaded, 1537

36. **Thomas Mylner**, King's messenger, beheaded,1537

37. **Sir Francis Bigod**, Leader of Bigods' Rebellion, executed, 1537

38. **Adam Sedbar**, Abbot of Jervaulx, hung, drawn and quartered 2nd June 1537 – plus the Abbots of Fountains, Bridlington and Gainsborough abbeys

39. **Thomas Fitzgerald**, 10th Earl of Kildare, and his five uncles, Beheaded, 1537

40. **John Forrest**, hung, drawn and quartered 22nd May 1538

41. **John Lambert**, hung, drawn and quartered 22nd November 1538

42. **Hugh Cook Faringdon**, Abbot of Reading Abbey, hung, drawn and quartered, Reading, 14th November 1539

43. **John Rugge**, an associate of, and co-accused with, Hugh Cook Faringdon, hung, drawn and quartered, Reading, 14th November 1539

44. **John Eynon**, Priest of St Giles Church, Reading, hung, drawn and quartered, Reading, 14th November 1539

45.   **Richard Whiting**, Abbot of Glastonbury, hung, drawn and quartered 22nd November 1539

46.   **John Thorne,** monk, hung, drawn and quartered 22nd November 1539

47.   **Roger James**, monk, hung, drawn and quartered 22nd November 1539

48.   **Robert Barnes,** burnt at the stake, 30th July 1540

49.   **William Jerome**, burnt at the stake, 30th July 1540

50.   **Thomas Garret**, burnt at the stake, 30th July 1540

51.   **Sir   Edward   Neville,** beheaded,   8th   December   1538

52.   **Henry Pole**, 1st Baron Montague, beheaded, 9th January 1539

53.   **Henry Courtenay Marquis of Exeter**, beheaded, 9th January 1539

54.   **Sir Nicholas Carew**, beheaded 3rd March 1539

55.   **Thomas Cromwell,** beheaded, 28th July 1540

56.   **Walter Hungerford,** beheaded, 28th July 1540

57.   **William Horne**, lay brother, Charterhouse, London, hung drawn and quartered, Tyburn, 4th August 1540

58.   **Robert Bird**, hung, drawn and quartered, 4th August 1540

59.   **Lawrence Cook**, Friar, hung, drawn and quartered, 4th August 1540

60.   **William Bird**, hung, drawn and quartered, 4th August 1540

61.   **Giles Heron**, hanged, August 1540

62.   **Margaret Pole**, Countess of Salisbury, beheaded, 27th May 1541

63.   **Lord Leonard Grey,** beheaded, Tower of London, 28th July 1541

64.   **Thomas Culpepper,** beheaded, 10th December 1541

65.   **Fancis Dearham**, hung, drawn and quartered, 10th December 1541

67.   **Catherine Howard**, beheaded, 13th February 1542

69.   **Jane Boleyn** (nee **Jane Parker**) Lady Rochford, beheaded, February1542

70.   **Henry   Pole   the   Younger**, disappeared in the Tower, 1542

71.   **Anne Askew**, & three others, burnt at the stake, 16th July 1546

72.   **Henry Howard**, Earl of Surrey, beheaded, 19th January 1547

Glossary

Attainder: Act of Parliament from the Norman French attaindre 'to convict'. In English law it was the legal consequence of sentence of death or outlawry in respect of treason or felony. Bills of Attainder and Bills of Pains and Penalties were enacted by Parliament attainting and punishing persons who had criminally offended against the state. Although originally used to supplement the punishment in a court of law, in 1459 they were used in their own right as a tool by the Lancastrians to destroy the Yorkists. These Bills were generally used in times of turbulence because of the peculiar nature of the offence or difficulties in applying the ordinary law. Accordingly, Bills were often passed against the accused person on evidence that would not have been sufficient in a court of law.

As Parliament was the highest court in the land the attainted person had no right to sue in a lower court.

The attainted person lost control of their property and could not carry out the duties or enjoy the privileges of a free person; but only in cases of treason were there forfeitures of entire estates; the attainted person's blood was held to be 'corrupted' and their descendents were disinherited. By 1504 some four hundred people had been attainted, although many were reversed by subsequent Parliaments. During the reign of Henry VIII people of the highest rank were brought to the scaffold by means of Bills of Attainder. Acts of Attainder were abolished in 1870.

Benvolences: These were forced loans or contributions levied by kings without legal

Authority; first levied by Edward IV in 1473 as a mark of 'good will' towards his rule; although similar 'free will' (but nevertheless compulsory) donations had not been uncommon in previous reigns. Richard III abolished them by Act of Parliament in 1484 as, "new and unlawful inventions", but irrespective of this he continued to exact them himself. They were widely used by Henry VII. In 1614 James I tried to raise money by this means but with little success. They were never used again by the Crown, Charles I expressly declining to do so.

Letters Patent: Literally, open letters, were royal commands and grants in a letter from the Monarch with his or her seal appended.

Oyer and Terminer: From ouir to hear, and terminer to determine. This was a form of assize or court sitting where a commission of Oyer and Terminer applied to a case where the indictment is heard by the commissioners. Commissions of Oyer and Terminer were used where quick action was needed, for example in cases of rebellion or political crises.

Peerage: the English peerage was formalised in the 15th century out of the earlier baronage. Peers temporal were those with an hereditary right to be summoned to parliament. Peers spiritual are those clergy who enjoy the same right. Compared to continental aristocrats English peers enjoyed few formal privileges, no exemption from taxation for example, as enjoyed by the French up until the Revolution. Peers had a right to be tried for criminal charges by other Peers up until 1948.

The main ranks of the Peerage were:

• **Duke**. The highest in rank. The word derives from the Latin dux, leader. The title was first conferred by Edward III on the Prince of Wales, Edward the Black Prince in 1337 when he was made Duke of Cornwall. The rank was exclusively intended for princes of the royal blood until Richard II extended its use. The second youngest son of the reigning Monarch is Duke of York. Henry VIII made his illegitimate son, Henry Fitzroy Duke of Richmond and Somerset, the only Dukedom to encompass two counties. The last non-royal Duke to be created was Arthur Wellesley who was created Duke of Wellington in 1814.

• **Marquis.** Second highest Peerage title; first bestowed in England the late fourteenth century.

- **Earl.** The third highest rank in the Peerage. In old English the word derived from the Danish for 'under-King'. It was used by the Normans as equivalent to the continental title of Count. Those enjoying the title were hereditary noblemen with administrative and military duties in shires.

- **Viscount.** Peerage title fourth in rank between Earl and Baron. The title was first created in the reign of Henry VI in 1440.

- **Baron.** The lowest rank in the hereditary Peerage. Originally Barons held military office or other post from the king or a great lord. Later the term came to apply to those who attended the king's council, or from the time of Henry III those who attended the newly created Parliament (1265 onwards). The term then came to mean a peer or lord who sat in Parliament (House of Lords). The creation of Barons by patent began under Richard II (1377-1399). Nowadays new Life Peers are Barons created by prime ministers mainly to reward MPs who have spent a political life-time fawning to their political party bosses; or to rich people who buy them by means of large donations to political parties; sometimes they are also granted to notables from the world of show business etc. as a sop to modern celebrity culture.

Praemunire: The word means to summon, and derives from the opening Latin word of the Writ ordering a Sheriff to summon offenders. It came to be used regarding Acts of Parliament to prevent judgements given in English courts being referred to courts outside the realm. The first Act was in 1353. The second Act of 1365 explicitly covers appeals to the Papacy. The Statute of Provisors 1393, sometimes known as the Great Statute of Praemunire imposed further constraints on communications with the Papacy. The laws of Praemunire were repealed in 1967 prior to Britain joining the European Economic Community. Appeals to the

European Court of Justice, and the European Court of Human Rights, would have been treason (as indeed some would argue they still are).

Privy Councillor: Prior to Henry VIII monarchs had royal councillors who were called 'privy (private) councillors' but there were no privy councils as such. Under Henry VIII a formalised Privy Council of key advisors did emerge from the larger Kings Council. This model continued until Charles I when it became too large for effective decision making. After the Restoration (1660) power increasingly devolved to specialised departments, e.g. the Treasury, Admiralty, etc. These evolved into the government departments of today. The Privy Council still exists to advise the Sovereign on Orders in Council, and the issuing of Royal Proclamations, and in times of crisis. Membership consists of all those chosen for cabinet posts in the past, and eminent people from the monarchical countries of the Commonwealth. All privy councillors swear an oath of loyalty to the Monarch. Some existing privy councillors have also served as European Commissioners, and have sworn an oath of loyalty to the European Union: this is incompatible and indeed treason.

End Notes

1: The Reign of Henry VIII, Personalities and Politics. David Starkey. Published by Collins and Brown. 1991. Page 11

2: The Wisdom of Psychopaths, Professor Kevin Dutton. Published by Scientific American/Farrar, Straus and Groux. 2013

3: A Medical History of the Kings and Queens of England. Clifford Brewer TD.F.R.C.S. Page 102

4: The Historical Journal, A new explanation for the reproductive woes and midlife decline of Henry VIII. Caterina Banks Whitely and Kyra Krammer. 2011

5: Journal of the Royal Society of Medicine, December 2009. 500 Years Later: Henry VIII, leg ulcers and the course of history. CR Chalmers and EJ Chaloner,

6: Journal of the Royal Society of Medicine, December 2009. 500 Years Later: Henry VIII, leg ulcers and the course of history. CR Chalmers and EJ Chaloner,

7: A Medical History of the Kings and Queens of England. Clifford Brewer TD.F.R.C.S. Page 103

8: Life of Henry VIII. Edward Hall or Halle. 1904

9: The Royal Bastards of Medieval England. Chris Given-Wilson & Alice Curteis. Routledge & Kegan Paul. 1984. Page 150

10: Chambers Encyclopaedia 1908 Edition. Fr-Hu. Page 648.

11: Green's short history of the English People. 1878

12: The Reign of Henry VIII. Personalities and Politics. By David Starkey. Published by Collins and Brown. 1991

13: Henry VIII and His Court. Neville Williams. Published by Weidenfeld and Nicholson Ltd. 1971

14: Richard III. Paul Murray Kendall. Published by George Allen & Unwin Ltd. 1955

15: The Other Tudors. Henry VIII's Mistresses and Bastards. By Philippa Jones. New Holland Publishers Ltd. 2009. Page 61

16: Henry VIII and His Court. Neville Williams. Published by Weidenfeld and Nicholson Ltd. 1971. Page 216

17: Thomas Cromwell. The rise and fall of Henry VIII's most notorious minister. By Robert Hutchinson. Published by Phoenix. 2008. Page 57

18: Thomas Cromwell. The rise and fall of Henry VIII's most notorious minister. By Robert Hutchinson. Published by Phoenix. 2008. Page 66

19: Thomas Cromwell. The rise and fall of Henry VIII's most notorious minister. By Robert Hutchinson. Published by Phoenix. 2008. Page 68

20: Chambers Encyclopaedia 1908 Edition. Dr-Fr. Page 644

21: Chambers Encyclopaedia 1908 Edition. Ro-Sw. Page 481

22: A Man of Singular Virtue. William Roper. Edited by A.L. Rowse. Published by The Folio Society. 1980. Page 28

23: Chambers Encyclopaedia 1908 Edition. Ma-Pe. Page 305

24: A Man of Singular Virtue. William Roper. Edited by A.L. Rowse. Published by The Folio Society. 1980. Page 60

25: History of the British Empire by William Francis Collier. Published by T. Nelson & Co. 1878. Page 224

26: Thomas More. James McConica, Published by The National Portrait Gallery. 1977. Page 50.

27: Bastard Prince. Henry VIII's Lost Son. Beverly A. Murphy. Published by Sutton Publishing. 2001. Page23

28: Henry VIII and His Court. Neville Williams. Published by Weidenfeld and Nicholson Ltd. 1971. Page 107

29: Thomas Cromwell. The rise and fall of Henry VIII's most notorious minister. By Robert Hutchinson. Published by Phoenix. 2008. Page 37

30: Henry VIII and His Court. Neville Williams. Published by Weidenfeld and Nicholson Ltd. 1971 page 127

31: Henry VIII and His Court. Neville Williams. Published by Weidenfeld and Nicholson Ltd. 1971 page 121

32: Thomas Cromwell. The rise and fall of Henry VIII's most notorious minister. By Robert Hutchinson. Published by Phoenix. 2008. Page 79

33: Chambers Encyclopaedia 1908 Edition. Be-Ca. Page 276

34: Henry VIII and His Court. Neville Williams. Published by Weidenfeld and Nicholson Ltd. 1971 page 142

35: Henry VIII and His Court. Neville Williams. Published by Weidenfeld and Nicholson Ltd. 1971 page 144-145

36: Thomas Cromwell. The rise and fall of Henry VIII's most notorious minister. By Robert Hutchinson. Published by Phoenix. 2008. Page 88

37: Thomas Cromwell. The rise and fall of Henry VIII's most notorious minister. By Robert Hutchinson. Published by Phoenix. 2008. Page 88

38: Thomas Cromwell. The rise and fall of Henry VIII's most notorious minister. By Robert Hutchinson. Published by Phoenix. 2008. Page 88

39: The Reign of Henry VIII. Personalities and Politics. By David Starkey. Published by Collins and Brown. 1991. Page 70

40: Pa Henry VIII and His Court. Neville Williams. Published by Weidenfeld and Nicholson Ltd. 1971 page 145

41: The Reign of Henry VIII. Personalities and Politics. By David Starkey. Published by Collins and Brown. 1991. Page 126

42: Chambers Encyclopaedia 1908 Edition. Volume Di-Fr Page 494.

43: Chambers Encyclopaedia 1908 Edition. Volume A-Ba Page 767.

44: Thomas Cromwell. The rise and fall of Henry VIII's most notorious minister. By Robert Hutchinson. Published by Phoenix. 2008. Page 167

45: Thomas Cromwell. The rise and fall of Henry VIII's most notorious minister. By Robert Hutchinson. Published by Phoenix. 2008. Page 180

46: Blessed Richard Whiting. The Catholic Encyclopaedia by Gilbert Huddleston. Vol 13. Published by The Robert Appleton Company, New York 1912.

47: Thomas Cromwell. The rise and fall of Henry VIII's most notorious minister. By Robert Hutchinson. Published by Phoenix. 2008. Page 104

48: Thomas Cromwell. The rise and fall of Henry VIII's most notorious minister. By Robert Hutchinson. Published by Phoenix. 2008. Page 115

49: Thomas Cromwell. The rise and fall of Henry VIII's most notorious minister. By Robert Hutchinson. Published by Phoenix. 2008. Page 115

50: Thomas Cromwell. The rise and fall of Henry VIII's most notorious minister. By Robert Hutchinson. Published by Phoenix. 2008. Page 116

51: Henry VIII and His Court. Neville Williams. Published by Weidenfeld and Nicholson Ltd. 1971 page 155

52: Thomas Cromwell. The rise and fall of Henry VIII's most notorious minister. By Robert Hutchinson. Published by Phoenix. 2008. Page 116

53: Thomas Cromwell. The rise and fall of Henry VIII's most notorious minister. By Robert Hutchinson. Published by Phoenix. 2008. Page 118

54: Thomas Cromwell. The rise and fall of Henry VIII's most notorious minister. By Robert Hutchinson. Published by Phoenix. 2008. Page 177

55: Thomas Cromwell. The rise and fall of Henry VIII's most notorious minister. By Robert Hutchinson. Published by Phoenix. 2008. Page 178

56: Thomas Cromwell. The rise and fall of Henry VIII's most notorious minister. By Robert Hutchinson. Published by Phoenix. 2008. Page 178

57: Henry VIII and His Court. Neville Williams. Published by Weidenfeld and Nicholson Ltd. 1971.

58: The Reign of Henry VIII. Personalities and Politics. By David Starkey. Published by Collins and Brown. 1991. Page 128

59: The Other Tudors. Henry VIII's Mistresses and Bastards. By Philippa Jones. New Holland Publishers (UK) Ltd. 2012. Page 280.

60: The Other Tudors. Henry VIII's Mistresses and Bastards. By Philippa Jones. New Holland Publishers (UK) Ltd. 2012. Page 282.

61: Henry VIII and His Court. Neville Williams. Published by Weidenfeld and Nicholson Ltd. 1971 page 208.

62: Henry VIII and His Court. Neville Williams. Published by Weidenfeld and Nicholson Ltd. 1971 page 209.

63: Henry VIII and His Court. Neville Williams. Published by Weidenfeld and Nicholson Ltd. 1971 page 210

64: The Royal Bastards of Medieval England. Chris Given-Wilson & Alice Curteis. Published by Routledge & Kegan Pau. 1984

65: The Other Tudors. Henry VIII's Mistresses and Bastards. By Philippa Jones. New Holland Publishers (UK) Ltd. 2012. Page 266.

66: The Other Tudors. Henry VIII's Mistresses and Bastards. By Philippa Jones. New Holland Publishers (UK) Ltd. 2012. Page 273

67: The Royal Bastards of Medieval England. Chris Given-Wilson & Alice Curteis. Published by Routledge & Kegan Pau. 1984

68: The Reign of Henry VIII. Personalities and Politics. By David Starkey. Published by Collins and Brown. 1991. Page 150

69: The Reign of Henry VIII. Personalities and Politics. By David Starkey. Published by Collins and Brown. 1991. Page 158

70: History of the British Empire by William Francis Collier. Published by T. Nelson & Co. 1878. Page 235

71: Henry VIII and His Court. Neville Williams. Published by Weidenfeld and Nicholson Ltd. 1971 page 255

72: Thomas Wolsey. His life and death. By George Cavendish. Published by the Folio Society. 1962. Page 31

73: Thomas Wolsey. His life and death. By George Cavendish. Published by the Folio Society. 1962. Page 39

74: Thomas Wolsey. His life and death. By George Cavendish. Published by the Folio Society. 1962. Page 39

75: The Other Tudors. Henry VIII's Mistresses and Bastards. By Philippa Jones. New Holland Publishers (UK) Ltd. 2012. Page 287.

76: The Reign of Henry VIII. Personalities and Politics. By David Starkey. Published by Collins and Brown. 1991. Page 144

77: Thomas Cromwell. The rise and fall of Henry VIII's most notorious minister. By Robert Hutchinson. Published by Phoenix. 2008. Page 70

78: Thomas Cromwell. The rise and fall of Henry VIII's most notorious minister. By Robert Hutchinson. Published by Phoenix. 2008. Page 147

79: Holbein in England. By Susan Foister, with contributions by Tim Batchelor. Published by Tate Publishing, a division of Tate Enterprises Ltd. 2006. Page 150

80: The Monarchy. Fifteen hundred years of British tradition. Edited by Robert Smith & John S. Moore. Published by Smith's Peerage Ltd. 1998. Page 158

81 Henry VIII and His Court. Neville Williams. Published by Weidenfeld and Nicholson Ltd. 1971. Page 258

82: The Monarchy. Fifteen hundred years of British tradition. Edited by Robert Smith & John S. Moore. Published by Smith's Peerage Ltd. 1998. Page 160

83: Making Faces, Using Forensic and Archaeological Evidence by John Prag and Richard Neave.

84: Published by the Trustees of the British Museum by the British Museum Press 1997.

85: The Princes in the Tower by Alison Weir. The Folio Society 1999. Page 236

About the Author

Gerard Batten is a Member of the European Parliament for London for the UK Independence Party. He was first elected in 2004, re-elected in 2009, and elected for a third term in May 2014.

He was a founder member of the UK Independence Party in 1993, and has served as a Party spokesman on Defence and Security, Immigration, and Home Affairs.

He has written articles and booklets on a wide range of political subjects and has two other books published by Bretwalda Press: Inglorious Revolution (2013), and The Road to Freedom (2014)

Inglorious Revolution was co-authored with Pavel Stroilov and charts how the English Constitution was subverted by Britain's membership of the European Union.

The Road to Freedom lays out the case for Britain's unconditional and unilateral withdrawal from the European Union.

This, his latest book, is his first foray into a purely historical subject and was written as light relief from the world of politics (or so he thought at the time of starting it).

www.BretwaldaBooks.com